The 30-Day Whole Food Cookbook For Beginners

900+ Days of Easy and Flavorful Recipes, Ignite Your Energy Levels, and Follow a Comprehensive 30-Day Meal Plan to Gain Optimal Health

By Isabella Sterling

Table Of Contents

CHAPTER 9: POULTRY PREPARATION

CHAPTER 10: FISH AND SEAFOOD

CHAPTER 11: HEALTHY SAUCES AND CONDIMENTS

Introduction

Introduction to the Whole30 Diet

Embarking on the Whole30 journey is akin to setting sail on a voyage of self-discovery and transformation. This 30-day adventure is more than a mere alteration in your diet; it's an immersive experience that reshapes your understanding of food and its profound impact on your body and mind. The Whole30 Diet, a brainchild of Dallas and Melissa Hartwig, emerged not as a fleeting trend in the vast ocean of dietary fads, but as a beacon of hope and health, a testament to the healing power of whole, unprocessed foods.

This diet is not a conventional one. It's a reset button for your body, a deliberate and conscious effort to eliminate certain food groups known to cause health issues in many people. The essence of the Whole30 Diet lies in its simplicity and its focus on mindfully consuming foods that nourish and rejuvenate. For thirty transformative days, you embark on a culinary journey that involves eliminating sugar, alcohol, grains, legumes, soy, and dairy. Instead, your plate becomes a canvas painted with vibrant vegetables, fruits, quality meats, seafood, eggs, nuts, and seeds.

The Whole30 Diet is as much a journey of discovery as it is of elimination. It invites you to explore the relationship between food and your physical and emotional well-being. It's about learning to appreciate the unadulterated flavors of nature, understanding the signals your body sends you, and responding with nourishment it genuinely needs.

As you navigate through these thirty days, expect to encounter challenges that test your resolve, habits, cravings, and emotional connections to food. Social pressures, the convenience of processed foods, and the rhythm of your existing lifestyle might seem like towering waves trying to sway your ship off course. Yet, it is within these challenges that the seeds of change and self-improvement are sown. Embracing these hurdles paves the way for personal growth and an enlightened understanding of your dietary needs.

The Whole30 Diet, though structured, allows for personal experimentation within its guidelines. It's a dance between discipline and creativity, requiring you to adhere to its principles while also encouraging you to explore the culinary possibilities within its framework. This dance leads to a deeper appreciation of the nuances of natural foods and the myriad ways they can be combined to create nourishing and delicious meals.

As your Whole30 journey nears its end, you'll likely notice profound changes in your body and mind. Increased energy, mental clarity, improved digestive health, and an overall sense of well-being are just a few of the rewards that await you. The conclusion of the thirty days marks not an end, but the beginning of a lifelong journey of conscious eating and understanding the unique needs of your body. This diet is a compass guiding you towards sustained health and wellness, a tool to forge a harmonious relationship with food, grounded in mindfulness and respect for your body's needs.

Importance of Whole Foods-Based Cooking

In a world where processed and fast foods are the norm, whole foods-based cooking is a rebellion against the status quo, a path less traveled that leads to improved health and wellness. It is about using ingredients that are minimally processed and as close to their natural form as possible. This approach to cooking and eating brings you closer to the source of your food, enabling you to experience the true taste, texture, and nutritional value that nature intended.

This way of cooking is more than just a technique; it's an art and a science. It's an art because it requires creativity and intuition to combine natural ingredients in a way that delights the palate. It's a science because it involves understanding the nutritional benefits of these ingredients and how they interact with your body. Whole foods-based cooking invites you to become an artist and a scientist in your kitchen, experimenting with flavors, textures, and colors to create meals that are as nourishing as they are delicious.

One of the key benefits of whole foods-based cooking is the control it gives you over what goes into your body. You become the gatekeeper of your health, selecting ingredients that contribute to your wellbeing. This style of cooking encourages you to read labels, understand what you're consuming, and make informed choices about the foods you prepare and eat.

Whole foods-based cooking also connects you with the rhythm of nature. It invites you to eat seasonally, to choose fresh, locally sourced produce, and to appreciate the abundance and diversity of the natural world. This connection brings a sense of harmony and balance, both in your diet and in your relationship with the environment.

Moreover, this approach to cooking and eating has a profound impact on your overall health. By consuming whole foods, you provide your body with essential nutrients in their most natural form, which are often lost or diminished in processed foods. This nutrient-rich diet supports your body's natural healing processes, boosts your immune system, improves digestion, and contributes to a feeling of vitality and energy.

Whole foods-based cooking is not just about the ingredients; it's about the process, the experience, and the intention behind each meal. It's about taking the time to prepare food with care, to savor each bite, and to share meals with loved ones. It's a celebration of food in its purest form, an act of self-care, and a commitment to nourishing your body and soul.

Chapter 1: Fundamentals of the Whole30 Diet

What Is the Whole30 Diet?

The Whole30 Diet is not merely about restricting certain foods; it's a holistic approach to eating that emphasizes the importance of quality, unprocessed foods. This program encourages you to consume foods that are nutrient-dense and minimally altered from their natural state. The philosophy behind Whole30 is rooted in the belief that certain food groups, while they may be perfectly healthy for some, could be having a negative impact on your health and fitness without you even realizing it.

The journey of the Whole30 Diet begins with a commitment. For thirty uninterrupted days, you embark on a culinary exploration, removing specific foods from your diet that are known to cause issues such as sugar spikes, gut irritations, inflammation, and addiction-like cravings. These include sugars, grains, dairy, legumes, and processed additives. The idea is not to permanently label these foods as 'bad', but to remove them temporarily and then reintroduce them methodically to understand their effects on your body.

During these thirty days, your diet will primarily consist of whole, unprocessed foods. Think fresh vegetables and fruits, grass-fed meats, seafood, eggs, nuts, and seeds. These foods are chosen for their nutritional value and their ability to positively impact your health. Whole30 places a strong emphasis on choosing high-quality meats and organic produce wherever possible, highlighting the importance of understanding the source of your food.

The Whole30 Diet is more than a set of eating guidelines; it's a tool for personal discovery and transformation. It's about learning to listen to your body, understanding what it needs, and how different foods affect you both physically and emotionally. This program is not just a diet; it's a reset for your entire system, a way to break unhealthy patterns and establish a healthier relationship with food.

One of the key aspects of Whole30 is its strict no-cheating policy. The program's creators emphasize that even a small amount of off-plan foods can disrupt the reset process, and hence, they encourage complete adherence for the full thirty days. This might seem daunting, but it's an integral part of the program's effectiveness. It's about giving your body a complete break from foods that could be causing issues and observing how your body responds in their absence.

Whole30 also differs from many other diets in that it's not about counting calories or macronutrients. There are no specific portions or calorie counts to follow. Instead, the focus is on eating whole, nutritious foods until you are satiated. This approach encourages a more intuitive way of eating, tuning into your body's natural hunger and fullness cues.

Throughout the Whole30 journey, you may experience a range of physical and emotional changes. The initial phase might include withdrawal-like symptoms as your body adjusts to the absence of sugar and processed foods. However, as you progress, most people report increased energy levels, clearer skin, improved digestion, and even a reduction in cravings for sugar and processed foods.

As you approach the end of the thirty days, the program guides you through a carefully planned reintroduction phase. This is where you gradually reintroduce the eliminated food groups, one at a time, while observing your body's responses. This phase is critical as it helps you understand which foods you might want to permanently eliminate or reduce in your diet and which ones you can consume without issues.

Health Benefits of the Whole30 Diet

The most immediate and noticeable benefit many people experience is a significant improvement in overall energy levels. The elimination of sugar and processed foods from your diet results in a more stable blood sugar level throughout the day. This stability helps to eliminate the highs and lows that lead to energy crashes and fatigue, replacing them with a consistent, steady flow of energy.

Digestive health sees a marked improvement on the Whole30 Diet. By cutting out foods that are known to cause gut irritation and inflammation, such as grains, dairy, and legumes, many individuals report a decrease in bloating, gas, and irregularities. This is a clear indication of a happier, healthier digestive system, which is crucial for overall health.

One of the most celebrated benefits of the Whole30 Diet is its impact on weight management. While weight loss is not the primary goal of the diet, it often occurs as a natural side effect of cutting out processed foods and sugars and focusing on nutrient-dense whole foods. More importantly, this weight management is sustainable, as the diet promotes a healthier relationship with food and a better understanding of satiety cues.

For many, the Whole30 Diet brings about significant improvements in skin clarity and texture. The diet's emphasis on hydration, along with the elimination of sugar and dairy – known contributors to skin issues like acne – often results in clearer, more radiant skin. This physical change is a powerful testament to the diet's positive impact on your body.

Mental clarity and improved cognitive function are also key benefits of this diet. The Whole30 Diet's focus on high-quality proteins, healthy fats, and a wide variety of vegetables provides your brain with the nutrients it needs to function optimally. Many people report a reduction in brain fog, improved concentration, and a sharper mind.

The diet also has a positive impact on emotional well-being and mood stability. The stabilizing effect on blood sugar levels helps in reducing mood swings and irritability, often associated with fluctuating sugar levels. This stability is complemented by an increased intake of omega-3 fatty acids from sources like fish and flax seeds, which are known to improve mood and reduce anxiety.

Another significant benefit is the potential reduction in inflammation. Chronic inflammation is linked to a host of health problems, and by eliminating foods that are known to cause inflammation, the Whole30 Diet can help in reducing the risk of various chronic diseases. This is particularly beneficial for individuals with autoimmune conditions or inflammatory disorders.

Lastly, the Whole30 Diet offers a unique opportunity to identify food sensitivities and allergies. The reintroduction phase is crucial in this respect, as it allows you to methodically reintroduce foods and observe how your body reacts to them. This can lead to a deeper understanding of any adverse reactions you may have to certain foods, helping you make more informed dietary choices in the future.

How the Whole30 Program Works

The foundation of this journey is its straightforward rule: for 30 days, you eliminate certain food groups from your diet. These include sugars, grains, dairy, legumes, alcohol, and processed additives, all known to potentially cause health issues like inflammation, digestive disturbances, and energy imbalances. This elimination phase is about discovery rather than deprivation, identifying how these foods affect you.

As you begin, the program encourages focusing not just on what you're eliminating but also on what you're incorporating into your diet. This includes a variety of fresh vegetables, fruits, quality meats, seafood, eggs, nuts, and seeds. Chosen for their nutritional value, these foods nourish and satisfy, supporting overall health.

A key element of the program is its emphasis on whole, unprocessed foods. This means selecting foods in their most natural state, free from additives, preservatives, and artificial ingredients. By doing so, you're nurturing your body with the highest quality fuel.

Throughout the 30 days, the program encourages mindfulness and attentiveness to your body's responses to these dietary changes. You may notice shifts in energy, mood, digestive health, and sleep patterns. This awareness is crucial, as it helps develop a deeper understanding of your body's needs and responses.

The program stresses the importance of not focusing on weight loss. Instead, it aims to shift your focus from weight to overall health and well-being. It's about changing your relationship with food and your body.

A significant aspect of the program is its rule against cheat days or slip-ups. The rationale is that even a small amount of non-compliant foods can disrupt the body's reset process. This strict adherence is what makes the program effective in identifying how certain foods impact your health.

As the 30-day period concludes, the program introduces a carefully planned reintroduction phase. This involves gradually bringing back the eliminated food groups, one at a time, and observing your body's responses. This process is vital in identifying food sensitivities or intolerances and understanding how different foods affect you.

What to Avoid and What to Eat

The essence of this diet is rooted in the consumption of fresh, natural, and unprocessed ingredients. At the heart of your meals are vegetables, both leafy greens and a vibrant array of others, offering a wealth of nutrients and fibers. Fruits, while included, are enjoyed in moderation due to their natural sugar content. They bring a natural sweetness and a variety of essential vitamins and antioxidants to your diet.

Proteins play a pivotal role in this diet, with a focus on lean meats like chicken, turkey, and lean cuts of beef. Seafood, including fish like salmon and trout, rich in omega-3 fatty acids, is also a staple, contributing to heart health and cognitive function. Eggs, versatile and nutrient-dense, are a cornerstone, perfect for any meal.

Nuts and seeds bring in healthy fats and are ideal for snacking or adding crunch and flavor to dishes. However, it's important to note that peanuts, classified as legumes, are not part of this dietary plan. Instead, options like almonds, cashews, and sunflower seeds are embraced.

Healthy fats are not shunned but celebrated for their role in satiety and overall health. Olive oil, coconut oil, and ghee are recommended for cooking and dressing foods. These fats are crucial for absorbing fat-soluble vitamins and providing essential fatty acids.

Foods to Set Aside

The foods excluded in this program are those that potentially cause inflammation, digestive issues, and imbalances in blood sugar. Grains, whether refined or whole, are set aside. This includes wheat, rice, oats, barley, and corn, along with all products derived from them.

Dairy products are also eliminated. This means saying a temporary goodbye to milk, cheese, yogurt, and butter. The objective is to assess how dairy affects your body once it's reintroduced later.

Legumes are another group to avoid. Beans, lentils, chickpeas, and soy, including tofu and soy milk, are excluded. While nutritious, they can be problematic for some people and are therefore omitted during this reset period.

Added sugars, whether natural or artificial, are not part of this diet. This exclusion is a crucial step in breaking the cycle of sugar dependence and stabilizing blood sugar levels. It involves avoiding not just obvious sweets but also checking labels for hidden sugars in packaged foods.

Alcohol, in all forms, is set aside. Its impact on liver health and blood sugar levels, along with its potential to disrupt healthy eating habits, makes it unsuitable for this period of dietary reset.

Lastly, processed foods and additives, including carrageenan, MSG, and sulfites, are avoided. The focus is on eating foods in their most natural and unadulterated state.

Chapter 2: Preparation and Planning

Tips for Whole30 Diet Planning

Before diving into meal planning, it's essential to have a clear understanding of the Whole30 guidelines. Knowing which foods to include and which to avoid is the foundation upon which your meal plan is built. Familiarize yourself with the diverse range of vegetables, fruits, proteins, nuts, seeds, and healthy fats that will form the core of your meals.

Meal Planning Strategies

1. **Weekly Meal Plans**: Start by planning your meals on a weekly basis. This allows for enough flexibility to accommodate unexpected changes and preferences, while still providing structure. Outline your meals for each day, including breakfast, lunch, dinner, and any snacks.

2. **Balancing Nutrition**: Each meal should be a balanced composition of protein, vegetables, and healthy fats. This balance is crucial not just for nutritional completeness but also for ensuring satiety and maintaining energy levels throughout the day.

3. **Batch Cooking and Prepping**: One of the most effective strategies for staying on track is to prepare meals in batches. Cook larger portions of dishes that can be stored and eaten over several days. This is especially useful for busy weekdays when time is limited. Similarly, prepping ingredients in advance – such as chopping vegetables or marinating proteins – can save time and simplify meal preparation.

4. **Embracing Variety**: While it's easy to fall into a routine of eating the same meals, variety is key to keeping your diet interesting and enjoyable. Experiment with different recipes and flavors. Try new vegetables, experiment with herbs and spices, and vary your protein sources.

5. **Smart Shopping**: Planning goes hand in hand with smart grocery shopping. Create a shopping list based on your meal plan, and stick to it. This not only helps in avoiding impulse purchases of non-compliant items but also ensures you have all the necessary ingredients for your meals.

6. **Planning for Challenges**: Anticipate and plan for challenging situations. This could include busy days when cooking is not feasible, social events, or eating out. Having a strategy for these scenarios will help you stay compliant and reduce stress.

7. **Utilizing Resources**: There are numerous resources available for Whole30 participants, from cookbooks and online recipes to meal planning apps and community forums. Leverage these resources for inspiration and guidance.

8. **Reflecting and Adjusting**: Finally, reflect on your meal plan at the end of each week. What worked well? What didn't? Use these insights to adjust your plan for the following week, continuously refining your approach to find what works best for you.

How to create a Weekly Meal Plan

Creating a weekly meal plan is more than just a logistical task; it's a creative process that ensures your diet remains diverse, balanced, and in line with Whole30 principles. Here's how you can approach this task effectively:

1. **Start with a Template**: Begin by creating a template for your week. This template should have slots for each meal of the day - breakfast, lunch, dinner, and possibly snacks. The idea is to fill these slots with different meals while ensuring nutritional balance and variety.

2. **Incorporate Diversity**: To prevent monotony, plan for different types of meals throughout the week. Mix and match proteins, vegetables, and healthy fats. For instance, if you have chicken for dinner one day, consider fish or beef the next. Similarly, rotate your vegetables and cooking styles to keep things interesting.

3. **Use Theme Nights**: One fun way to add variety is by having theme nights. For example, "Mexican Monday" could feature a Whole30-compliant taco salad, while "Italian Wednesday" could be a zucchini noodle and meatball night. These themes can add an element of excitement and anticipation to your meals.

4. **Plan for Leftovers**: Cook in quantities that ensure you have leftovers. This strategy is especially useful for lunches, where leftovers can easily be repurposed from the previous night's dinner, saving time and reducing food waste.

5. **Snack Wisely**: If you plan to include snacks, choose them wisely. Opt for simple options like a handful of nuts, some carrot sticks with Whole30-compliant dip, or a piece of fruit. Remember, snacking is not a central part of Whole30, so keep it minimal and only as needed.

6. **Be Realistic and Flexible**: Your meal plan needs to be practical and adaptable. Consider your weekly schedule – busy workdays, social commitments, and family activities – and plan accordingly. Quick and easy meals can be slotted for your busiest days.

7. **Prep in Advance**: Once your meal plan is ready, dedicate time over the weekend for meal prep. This can include washing and chopping vegetables, marinating proteins, or fully preparing some meals ready for reheating. The more you prepare in advance, the easier your week will be.

8. **Shopping List Alignment**: Align your meal plan with your shopping list. This ensures you buy exactly what you need, reducing the chances of impulse buys and ensuring you don't fall short on essential ingredients during the week.

9. **Adapt and Overcome**: Be prepared to adapt your meal plan as needed. Life is unpredictable, and flexibility is key. If you find yourself unable to cook one evening, have a list of Whole30-compliant emergency options, like a simple salad with canned tuna or a quick stir-fry with whatever vegetables you have.

Creating a weekly meal plan is a cornerstone of success on the Whole30 journey. It ensures that you have a diverse, delicious, and compliant menu lined up every day, reducing daily decision fatigue and keeping you on track. By planning ahead, you empower yourself to navigate the Whole30 journey with confidence and ease.

Chapter 3: Breakfast Recipes

Avocado and Spinach Power Omelette

- **P.T.**: 15 mins
- **Ingr.**: Trio of eggs, ½ ripe avocado (sliced), cupful of fresh spinach, spoonful of olive oil, seasoning to taste.
- **Servings**: 1
- **Process**:
  1. Warm olive oil in a pan over medium flame.
  2. Beat eggs with seasoning in a bowl.
  3. Pour eggs into pan, ensuring even spread.
  4. As eggs set, place spinach and avocado slices on one side.
  5. Gently fold and continue heating until eggs are fully cooked.
- **Shopping List**: Eggs, avocado, fresh spinach, olive oil.
- **Tips**: A non-stick pan simplifies the flipping process.

Coconut Yogurt Parfait

- **P.T.**: 10 mins
- **Ingr.**: Cup of coconut yogurt, ½ cup mixed berries, handful of almond slivers, spoonful of chia seeds.
- **Servings**: 1
- **Process**:
  1. Layer half the yogurt in a glass.
  2. Add a layer of berries, almonds, and chia.
  3. Repeat layering.
- **Shopping List**: Coconut yogurt, mixed berries, almond slivers, chia seeds.
- **Tips**: Assemble the night prior for a quick morning start.

Herb-Infused Scrambled Eggs

- **P.T.**: 10 mins
- **Ingr.**: Quartet of eggs, tablespoon of chopped herbs (basil, parsley, chives), double teaspoons of ghee, seasoning.
- **Servings**: 2
- **Process**:
    1. Whisk eggs with herbs and seasoning.
    2. Melt ghee in skillet over medium flame.
    3. Cook the egg mixture, stirring gently.
- **Shopping List**: Eggs, fresh herbs, ghee.
- **Tips**: Blend of herbs enhances flavor complexity.

Banana Almond Smoothie Bowl

- **P.T.**: 10 mins
- **Ingr.**: Pair of ripe bananas, cup of almond milk, duo tablespoons almond butter, spoonful of flaxseeds.
- **Servings**: 1
- **Process**:
    1. Blend bananas, almond milk, and almond butter to smooth consistency.
    2. Transfer to bowl and garnish with flaxseeds.
- **Shopping List**: Bananas, almond milk, almond butter, flaxseeds.
- **Tips**: Chill bananas prior for a denser smoothie.

Tomato Basil Frittata

- **P.T.**: 20 mins
- **Ingr.**: Half dozen eggs, cup of halved cherry tomatoes, quarter cup chopped basil, spoonful of olive oil, seasoning.
- **Servings**: 2-3
- **Process**:
  1. Preheat oven to 350°F (175°C).
  2. Combine eggs with seasoning and basil.
  3. Sauté tomatoes in olive oil in an oven-proof skillet, add egg mixture.
  4. Cook for 5 mins, then bake for 10-15 mins.
- **Shopping List**: Eggs, cherry tomatoes, basil, olive oil.
- **Tips**: Confirm skillet's oven compatibility before baking.

Smashed Avocado Toast

- **P.T.**: 15 mins
- **Ingr.**: Single avocado, duo slices of Whole30-compliant bread, teaspoon of lemon juice, seasoning, spoonful of olive oil.
- **Servings**: 1-2
- **Process**:
  1. Toast bread slices.
  2. Mash avocado with lemon juice and seasoning.
  3. Spread over toast, then drizzle with olive oil.
- **Shopping List**: Avocado, Whole30-compliant bread, lemon, olive oil.
- **Tips**: Enhance with red pepper flakes for a spicy kick.

Broccoli and Egg Muffins

- **P.T.**: 30 mins
- **Ingr.**: Half dozen eggs, cup of chopped broccoli, quarter cup diced onion, spoonful of olive oil, seasoning.
- **Servings**: 6 muffins

- **Process**:
  1. Oven preheating to 350°F (175°C), muffin tin prepped.
  2. Sauté broccoli and onion in oil, cool afterward.
  3. Mix eggs with seasoning, stir in broccoli mixture.
  4. Allocate into muffin tin, bake for 20-25 mins.
- **Shopping List**: Eggs, broccoli, onion, olive oil.
- **Tips**: Suitable for meal prep, refrigerate for up to 4 days.

Spicy Sweet Potato Hash

- **P.T.**: 25 mins
- **Ingr.**: Pair of medium sweet potatoes (diced), single red bell pepper (diced), onion (diced), double teaspoons paprika, spoonful of olive oil, seasoning.
- **Servings**: 2
- **Process**:
  1. Olive oil heated in skillet over medium flame.
  2. Add sweet potatoes, bell pepper, onion, paprika, and seasoning.
  3. Cook until vegetables tenderize.
- **Shopping List**: Sweet potatoes, red bell pepper, onion, paprika, olive oil.
- **Tips**: Complement with a fried egg for additional protein.

Coconut Chia Pudding

- **P.T.**: Overnight
- **Ingr.**: Quarter cup chia seeds, cup of coconut milk, tablespoon of maple syrup, half teaspoon vanilla extract.
- **Servings**: 2
- **Process**:
  1. Combine chia seeds, coconut milk, syrup, and vanilla in a bowl.
  2. Refrigerate overnight until pudding sets.
- **Shopping List**: Chia seeds, coconut milk, maple syrup, vanilla extract.
- **Tips**: Serve with fresh fruit for extra taste and nutrients.

Carrot and Walnut Breakfast Muffins

- **P.T.**: 35 mins
- **Ingr.**: Duo cups almond flour, cup of grated carrot, half cup chopped walnuts, trio of eggs, quarter cup olive oil, teaspoon of baking powder, teaspoon cinnamon.
- **Servings**: 12 muffins

- **Process**:
  1. Oven preheated to 350°F (175°C), muffin tin lined.
  2. Blend almond flour, baking powder, and cinnamon.
  3. In another bowl, whisk eggs and oil, mix in carrots and walnuts.
  4. Unite wet and dry ingredients, spoon into tin.
  5. Bake for 20-25 mins.
- **Shopping List**: Almond flour, carrots, walnuts, eggs, olive oil, baking powder, cinnamon.
- **Tips**: Store in an airtight container, refrigerate up to 5 days or freeze.

Almond Butter & Berry Chia Pudding

- **P.T.**: 15 mins (+ overnight chilling)
- **Ingr.**:
  - 3 tbsp chia seeds
  - 1 cup almond milk
  - 2 tbsp almond butter
  - 1 tbsp honey (optional)
  - 1/2 cup mixed berries

- **Servings**: 2
- **Process**:
  1. Combine chia seeds and almond milk in a bowl, stir well.
  2. Add almond butter, mix until well integrated.
  3. Refrigerate overnight until set.
  4. Top with mixed berries before serving.
- **Shopping List**: Chia seeds, almond milk, almond butter, mixed berries, honey (optional).
- **Tips**: For added sweetness, drizzle with honey or maple syrup. Customize with your favorite fruits or nuts.

Savory Spinach & Mushroom Omelet

- **P.T.**: 20 mins
- **Ingr.**:
  - 4 eggs
  - 1 cup fresh spinach
  - 1/2 cup mushrooms, sliced
  - 1 small onion, finely chopped
  - 2 tbsp olive oil
  - Salt and pepper to taste

- **Servings**: 2
- **Process**:
  1. Sauté mushrooms and onion in 1 tbsp olive oil until tender.
  2. Beat eggs, season with salt and pepper.

3. Pour eggs into a skillet, add spinach, cooked mushrooms, and onions.
4. Cook until eggs are set, then fold omelet.

- **Shopping List**: Eggs, fresh spinach, mushrooms, onion, olive oil.

- **Tips**: Serve with a side of avocado slices for a heartier meal.

Toasted Coconut & Quinoa Breakfast Bowl

- **P.T.**: 25 mins
- **Ingr.**:
    - 1/2 cup quinoa
    - 1 cup coconut milk
    - 2 tbsp toasted coconut flakes
    - 1/4 cup almonds, chopped
    - 1 banana, sliced
    - 1 tbsp honey (optional)
- **Servings**: 2
- **Process**:
    1. Cook quinoa in coconut milk until fluffy.
    2. Transfer to bowls, top with banana slices, toasted coconut, and almonds.
    3. Drizzle with honey if desired.

- **Shopping List**: Quinoa, coconut milk, coconut flakes, almonds, banana, honey (optional).
- **Tips**: Experiment with different fruits or nuts for variety. Can be served warm or cold.

Chapter 4: Healthy and Flavorful Salads

Mediterranean Magic Salad

- **P.T.:** 20 mins
- **Ingr.:** Duo cups of mixed greens, 1 cucumber (cubed), 1 bell pepper (cubed), handful of olives, duo tbsp extra virgin olive oil, tbsp of apple cider vinegar, mixed herbs (oregano, basil), sea salt, cracked pepper.
- **Servings**: 2
- **Process**:
  1. Tumble mixed greens, cucumber, bell pepper, and olives in a bowl.
  2. Whisk together olive oil, vinegar, herbs, salt, and pepper to create the dressing.
  3. Drizzle dressing over salad, toss to coat evenly.
- **Shopping List**: Mixed greens, cucumber, bell pepper, olives, olive oil, apple cider vinegar, herbs.
- **Tips**: Allow salad to meld for a brief period for intensified flavors.

Avocado Citrus Delight

1. Merge avocado, grapefruit, and orange in a salad bowl.
2. Blend lime juice, olive oil, honey, and salt for the dressing.
3. Gently toss the salad with the dressing, garnish with almond slices.

- **P.T.**: 15 mins
- **Ingr.**: Pair of avocados (sliced), 1 grapefruit (segments), 1 orange (segments), ¼ cup almond slices, dressing made of lime juice, olive oil, and a drizzle of honey, pinch of salt.
- **Servings**: 2
- **Process**:

- **Shopping List**: Avocados, grapefruit, orange, almonds, lime, olive oil, honey.
- **Tips**: Use a sharp blade to segment citrus for neat presentation.

Heirloom Tomato & Herb Salad

- **P.T.**: 10 mins
- **Ingr.**: 3 cups heirloom tomatoes (varied hues, sliced), quarter cup fresh basil (torn), duo tbsp chives (chopped), duo tbsp extra virgin olive oil, tbsp balsamic reduction, sea salt, pepper grindings.

- **Servings**: 2-3
- **Process**:
  1. Layout tomato slices on a serving dish.
  2. Scatter torn basil and snipped chives over tomatoes.

3. Drizzle with olive oil and balsamic, season to taste.

- **Shopping List**: Heirloom tomatoes, basil, chives, olive oil, balsamic vinegar.

- **Tips**: Mix tomato types for a visually striking dish.

Crunchy Kale & Apple Salad

- **P.T.**: 15 mins
- **Ingr.**: 4 cups kale (hand-torn), 1 apple (thinly sliced), ¼ cup walnut bits, duo tbsp lemon juice, trio tbsp olive oil, tbsp Dijon mustard, seasoning.
- **Servings**: 2
- **Process**:
    1. Tenderize kale with lemon juice and a pinch of sea salt.
    2. Add apple slices and walnut pieces to kale.
    3. Whisk together olive oil, mustard, and seasoning for dressing.
    4. Dress salad with prepared mixture.
- **Shopping List**: Kale, apple, walnuts, lemon, olive oil, Dijon mustard.
- **Tips**: Gentle massaging of kale softens its texture, enhances flavor.

Spicy Southwest Salad

- **P.T.**: 20 mins
- **Ingr.**: 2 cups of lettuce, cupful of black beans (cooked), cup of corn kernels, 1 avocado (cubed), 1 red onion (finely diced), juice of 1 lime, duo tbsp olive oil, tsp of cumin, seasoning, dash of cayenne.
- **Servings**: 2
- **Process**:
    1. Mix lettuce, black beans, corn, avocado chunks, and onion in a large bowl.
    2. Blend lime juice, olive oil, cumin, seasoning, and a hint of cayenne for the dressing.

3. Toss salad with prepared dressing.
- **Shopping List**: Lettuce, black beans, corn, avocado, red onion, lime, olive oil, cumin, cayenne pepper.

- **Tips**: Modify cayenne quantity for preferred heat level.

Cucumber Noodle Salad

- **P.T.**: 15 mins
- **Ingr.**: Pair of large cucumbers (spiralized), ¼ cup rice vinegar, tbsp sesame oil, tbsp soy sauce, tsp honey, tsp grated ginger, sprinkle of sesame seeds.

- **Servings**: 2
- **Process**:
  1. Place cucumber spirals in a salad bowl.
  2. For dressing, combine vinegar, sesame oil, soy sauce, honey, and ginger.
  3. Toss cucumber noodles with dressing, garnish with sesame seeds.
- **Shopping List**: Cucumbers, rice vinegar, sesame oil, soy sauce, honey, ginger, sesame seeds.
- **Tips**: Dry cucumber spirals with paper towels to avoid excess moisture.

Broccoli Almond Crunch Salad

- **P.T.**: 20 mins
- **Ingr.**: 3 cups broccoli florets (chopped), ¼ cup almond slices, ¼ cup dried cranberries, duo tbsp Whole30-compliant mayonnaise, tbsp apple cider vinegar, drizzle of honey, pinch of salt.
- **Servings**: 2-3
- **Process**:
  1. Briefly boil broccoli, then cool.
  2. Combine mayo, vinegar, honey, and salt for dressing.
  3. Toss broccoli with almonds and cranberries.
  4. Dress with prepared mixture.
- **Shopping List**: Broccoli, almonds, dried cranberries, mayonnaise, apple cider vinegar, honey.
- **Tips**: Blanching preserves broccoli's crunch and vibrant hue.

Sweet Potato & Pecan Salad

- **P.T.**: 25 mins
- **Ingr.**: Duo sweet potatoes (cubed, roasted), ½ cup pecans (toasted), duo cups arugula, dressing (lemon juice, olive oil, honey), seasoning.
- **Servings**: 2
- **Process**:
  1. Roast sweet potato cubes until fork-tender.
  2. Whisk lemon juice, olive oil, honey, salt, and pepper for dressing.
  3. Combine arugula, sweet potatoes, and pecans.
  4. Toss with dressing.
- **Shopping List**: Sweet potatoes, pecans, arugula, lemon, olive oil, honey.
- **Tips**: Pre-roasting sweet potatoes saves preparation time.

Carrot Ribbon & Avocado Salad

- **P.T.:** 15 mins
- **Ingr.:** Trio of large carrots (ribboned), 1 avocado (sliced), ¼ cup sunflower seeds, duo tbsp olive oil, tbsp lemon juice, drizzle of honey, sea salt, cracked pepper.

- **Servings**: 2
- **Process**:
  1. Ribbon carrots using a vegetable peeler.
  2. Whisk olive oil, lemon juice, honey, salt, and pepper to create dressing.
  3. Combine carrot ribbons with avocado slices and sunflower seeds.
  4. Toss with dressing.
- **Shopping List**: Carrots, avocado, sunflower seeds, olive oil, lemon, honey.
- **Tips**: Chilling the salad beforehand melds the flavors better.

Lemon Herb Chicken Salad

- **P.T.:** 30 mins
- **Ingr.:** Duo chicken breasts (grilled, sliced), trio cups mixed greens, ¼ cup cherry tomatoes, ¼ cup cucumber (sliced), dressing (lemon juice, olive oil, mixed herbs), seasoning.
- **Servings**: 2
- **Process**:

1. Grill chicken breasts, then slice.
2. Blend lemon juice, olive oil, herbs, salt, and pepper for dressing.
3. Toss greens, tomatoes, cucumber, and chicken with dressing.

- **Shopping List**: Chicken breasts, mixed greens, cherry tomatoes, cucumber, lemon, olive oil, herbs.

- **Tips**: Marinating chicken in lemon and herbs pre-grilling adds depth of flavor.

Roasted Beet & Arugula Salad

- **P.T.**: 30 mins
- **Ingr.**:
  - 3 medium beets, roasted and cubed
  - 2 cups arugula
  - 1/4 cup walnuts, toasted
  - 1/4 cup goat cheese, crumbled (optional)
  - 2 tbsp balsamic vinegar
  - 1 tbsp olive oil
  - Salt and pepper to taste
- **Servings**: 2
- **Process**:

1. Mix balsamic vinegar, olive oil, salt, and pepper for dressing.
2. Toss roasted beets, arugula, and walnuts in the dressing.
3. Sprinkle goat cheese on top (if using).

- **Shopping List**: Beets, arugula, walnuts, goat cheese (optional), balsamic vinegar, olive oil.
- **Tips**: Roast beets in advance to save time. They can be stored in the refrigerator for up to a week.

Quinoa & Black Bean Salad

- **P.T.**: 25 mins
- **Ingr.**:
  - 1 cup cooked quinoa
  - 1 can black beans, drained and rinsed
  - 1 red bell pepper, chopped
  - 1/2 red onion, finely chopped
  - 1/4 cup cilantro, chopped
  - 2 limes, juiced
  - 2 tbsp olive oil
  - Salt and pepper to taste
- **Servings**: 2
- **Process**:
  1. In a bowl, combine quinoa, black beans, bell pepper, onion, and cilantro.
  2. Whisk together lime juice, olive oil, salt, and pepper.
  3. Pour dressing over salad and toss.
- **Shopping List**: Quinoa, black beans, red bell pepper, red onion, cilantro, limes, olive oil.
- **Tips**: This salad can be made in advance and tastes better as the flavors meld.

Greek Chickpea Salad

- **P.T.**: 20 mins
- **Ingr.**:
  - 1 can chickpeas, drained and rinsed
  - 1 cucumber, diced
  - 1 tomato, diced
  - 1/2 red onion, finely chopped
  - 1/4 cup Kalamata olives, halved
  - 1/4 cup feta cheese, crumbled (optional)
  - 2 tbsp olive oil
  - 1 tbsp red wine vinegar
  - 1 tsp dried oregano
  - Salt and pepper to taste
- **Servings**: 2
- **Process**:

1. Combine chickpeas, cucumber, tomato, onion, and olives in a bowl.
2. In a separate bowl, mix olive oil, red wine vinegar, oregano, salt, and pepper.
3. Pour dressing over the salad and toss.
4. Sprinkle feta cheese on top (if using).

- **Shopping List**: Chickpeas, cucumber, tomato, red onion, Kalamata olives, feta cheese (optional), olive oil, red wine vinegar, oregano.
- **Tips**: Serve chilled for a refreshing meal. The salad can be stored in the refrigerator for up to two days.

Chapter 5: Nutrient-Rich Soups and Stews

Rustic Fowl & Root Vegetable Broth

- **P.T.**: 45 mins
- **Ingr.**: Pair of fowl breasts (cubed), triplet of carrots (sliced), duo of parsnips (sliced), singular onion (diced), 4 cups fowl broth, duo tsp thyme, tsp rosemary, drizzle of olive essence, sea salt, pepper dust.
- **Servings**: 4
- **Process**:
    1. In a saucepan, sauté onion in olive essence till golden.
    2. Brown the fowl cubes.
    3. Introduce carrots, parsnips, thyme, rosemary, seasoning.
    4. Cover with fowl broth, simmer till root veggies soften.
- **Shopping List**: Fowl breasts, carrots, parsnips, onion, fowl broth, thyme, rosemary, olive essence.
- **Tips**: A dash of lemon zest enhances the broth's aroma.

Spiced Lentil & Curly Kale Potage

- **P.T.**: 40 mins
- **Ingr.**: Cup of lentils, 3 cups curly kale (chopped), onion (diced), duo garlic cloves (minced), 4 cups vegetable stock, tsp cumin, tsp coriander, olive essence, sea salt, pepper.

- **Servings**: 4
- **Process**:
  1. Sauté onion and garlic in olive essence.
  2. Combine lentils, spices, seasoning.
  3. Douse with stock, boil, then reduce to simmer till lentils tenderize.
  4. Fold in curly kale till it wilts.
- **Shopping List**: Lentils, curly kale, onion, garlic, vegetable stock, cumin, coriander, olive essence.
- **Tips**: A squeeze of citrus adds a fresh dimension.

Hearty Ox & Sweet Tuber Soup

- **P.T.**: 1 hr
- **Ingr.**: 1 lb oxen stew meat (cubed), duo sweet tubers (cubed), singular onion (diced), 4 cups oxen broth, duo tsp paprika, olive essence, salt, pepper.
- **Servings**: 4
- **Process**:

1. Sear oxen cubes in olive essence, reserve.
2. Sauté onion.
3. Introduce sweet tubers, paprika, seasoning.
4. Return oxen, cover with broth, simmer till oxen tender.

- **Shopping List**: Oxen stew meat, sweet tubers, onion, oxen broth, paprika, olive essence.

- **Tips**: Uniform cubing ensures even cooking.

Creamed Cauliflower & Garlic Brew

P.T.: 35 mins

- **Ingr.**: Head of cauliflower (chopped), quartet garlic cloves, 3 cups vegetable stock, onion (diced), cup of coconut milk, duo tsp thyme, olive essence, salt, pepper.
- **Servings**: 4
- **Process**:
    1. Oven roast cauliflower and garlic till tanned.
    2. In a pot, glaze onion in olive essence, mix in roasted cauliflower and garlic.
    3. Lavish with stock, simmer for 20.
    4. Puree soup, reheat, stir in coconut milk.

- **Shopping List**: Cauliflower, garlic, vegetable stock, onion, coconut milk, thyme, olive essence.
- **Tips**: Roasting amplifies the cauliflower's nuttiness.

Moroccan Chickpea & Veg Medley

- **P.T.**: 50 mins
- **Ingr.**: Can of chickpeas (drained), duo carrots (sliced), singular zucchini (sliced), onion (diced), 4 cups vegetable stock, duo tsp cumin, tsp cinnamon, olive essence, salt, pepper.
- **Servings**: 4
-

- **Process**:
  1. Olive essence sauté of onion.
  2. Add carrots, zucchini, spices, seasoning.
  3. Introduce chickpeas and stock, simmer till veggies tender.
- **Shopping List**: Chickpeas, carrots, zucchini, onion, vegetable stock, cumin, cinnamon, olive essence.
- **Tips**: Top with fresh mint for a Moroccan touch.

Smoked Tomato & Capsicum Brew

- **P.T.**: 30 mins
- **Ingr.**: 4 cups tomato liquid, duo red capsicums (chopped), onion (diced), duo garlic cloves (minced), tsp smoked paprika, olive essence, salt, pepper.
- **Servings**: 4
- **Process**:
  1. Sauté onion and garlic in olive essence.
  2. Add capsicums, paprika, seasoning.
  3. Pour in tomato liquid, simmer for 20.
- **Shopping List**: Tomato liquid, red capsicums, onion, garlic, smoked paprika, olive essence.
- **Tips**: Blend for a silky texture post-cooking.

Ginger-Infused Gourd Soup

- **P.T.**: 40 mins
- **Ingr.**: 1 gourd (peeled, cubed), onion (diced), 4 cups vegetable stock, duo tsp ginger (grated), cup of coconut milk, olive essence, salt, pepper.
- **Servings**: 4
- **Process**:
  1. Sauté onion and ginger in olive essence.
  2. Stir in gourd, simmer in stock till soft.
  3. Blend to creaminess, reheat, infuse with coconut milk.
- **Shopping List**: Gourd, onion, vegetable stock, ginger, coconut milk, olive essence.
- **Tips**: A garnish of roasted seeds adds texture.

Zesty Fowl Citrus Soup

- **P.T.**: 50 mins
- **Ingr.**: Pair of fowl breasts (shredded), 4 cups fowl broth, onion (diced), duo carrots (sliced), 1 citrus (juice and zest), duo tsp thyme, olive essence, salt, pepper.
- **Servings**: 4
- **Process**:
    1. Poach fowl in broth, then shred.
    2. Glaze onion and carrots in olive essence.
    3. Blend fowl, broth, citrus elements, thyme, seasoning.
    4. Simmer till veggies soften.
- **Shopping List**: Fowl breasts, fowl broth, onion, carrots, citrus, thyme, olive essence.
- **Tips**: Citrus infusion at the culmination of cooking preserves its vibrant essence.

Spicy Sausage & Curly Kale Stew

- **P.T.**: 45 mins
- **Ingr.**: 1 lb spicy sausage (sliced), 3 cups curly kale (chopped), onion (diced), 4 cups fowl broth, duo tubers (cubed), tsp red pepper flakes, olive essence, salt, pepper.
- **Servings**: 4
- **Process**:
    1. Brown sausage slices in olive essence, set aside.
    2. Sauté onion in same vessel.
    3. Add tubers, broth, pepper flakes, seasoning, simmer till tubers yield.

4. Stir in sausage and curly kale, cook till kale softens.
- **Shopping List**: Spicy sausage, curly kale, onion, fowl broth, tubers, red pepper flakes, olive essence.
- **Tips**: Modify pepper flake quantity for heat preference.

Asian Mushroom & Tofu Broth

- **P.T.**: 35 mins
- **Ingr.**: Duo cups mushrooms (sliced), tofu block (cubed), 4 cups vegetable stock, onion (diced), duo garlic cloves (minced), duo tsp soy condiment, tsp sesame essence, spring onions (for garnish).
- **Servings**: 4
- **Process**:
  1. Sauté onion and garlic in sesame essence.
  2. Add mushrooms, cook till moisture seeps.
  3. Introduce tofu, stock, and soy condiment, simmer for 20.
  4. Garnish with chopped spring onions.
- **Shopping List**: Mushrooms, tofu, vegetable stock, onion, garlic, soy condiment, sesame essence, spring onions.
- **Tips**: Incorporate leafy greens like bok choy for an added nutrient boost.

Coconut Lentil Harmony Soup

- **P.T.:** 40 mins
- **Ingr.:**
    - 1 cup red lentils
    - 1 can coconut milk
    - 4 cups vegetable broth
    - 1 onion, diced
    - 2 carrots, diced
    - 2 garlic cloves, minced
    - 1 tbsp curry powder
    - 1 tsp turmeric
    - 2 tbsp olive oil
    - Salt and pepper to taste
- **Servings**: 4
- **Process**:

1. Sauté onion, carrots, and garlic in olive oil until softened.
2. Stir in curry powder and turmeric, cook for 1 minute.
3. Add lentils, coconut milk, and vegetable broth.
4. Simmer for 30 minutes or until lentils are soft.

- **Shopping List**: Red lentils, coconut milk, vegetable broth, onion, carrots, garlic, curry powder, turmeric, olive oil.
- **Tips**: Serve with a squeeze of lime juice for added zest.

Hearty Tuscan Kale & White Bean Stew

- **P.T.:** 50 mins
- **Ingr.:**
    - 2 cans white beans, drained and rinsed
    - 1 bunch Tuscan kale, chopped
    - 1 onion, chopped
    - 2 carrots, diced
    - 4 cups vegetable broth
    - 1 can diced tomatoes
    - 3 garlic cloves, minced
    - 1 tsp dried thyme
    - 2 tbsp olive oil
    - Salt and pepper to taste
- **Servings**: 4
- **Process**:

1. In a pot, sauté onion, carrots, and garlic in olive oil.
2. Add beans, tomatoes, kale, thyme, and vegetable broth.

3. Simmer for 40 minutes, stirring occasionally.

- **Shopping List**: White beans, Tuscan kale, onion, carrots, vegetable broth, canned tomatoes, garlic, thyme, olive oil.
- **Tips**: This stew thickens as it cools and is great for leftovers.

Spiced Butternut Squash Bisque

- **P.T.**: 45 mins
- **Ingr.**:
  - 1 medium butternut squash, peeled and cubed
  - 1 onion, diced
  - 3 cups vegetable broth
  - 1 apple, peeled and diced
  - 1 tsp cinnamon
  - 1/2 tsp nutmeg
  - 2 tbsp olive oil
  - Salt and pepper to taste

- **Servings**: 4
- **Process**:
  1. Roast butternut squash until tender.
  2. Sauté onion in olive oil until translucent.
  3. Blend roasted squash, onion, apple, and spices with broth until smooth.
  4. Heat bisque in a pot until warm.

- **Shopping List**: Butternut squash, onion, vegetable broth, apple, cinnamon, nutmeg, olive oil.
- **Tips**: Garnish with roasted pumpkin seeds for a crunchy texture.

Chapter 6: Vegetable-Based Side Dishes

Root Ensemble

1. Warmth at 400°F (200°C) preheated oven.
2. Tumble roots with olive essence, rosemary, sea salt, and pepper.
3. Lay out on baking tray, roast till tender.

- **Shopping List**: Sweet tubers, beetroots, parsnips, olive essence, rosemary.
- **Tips**: Shaking tray midway ensures even roasting.

- **P.T.**: 40 mins
- **Ingr.**: Pair of sweet tubers (cubed), trio of beetroots (cubed), duo of parsnips (sliced), spoonful of olive essence, pinch of rosemary, sea salt, crushed pepper.
- **Servings**: 4
- **Process**:

Cauliflower Planks

- **P.T.**: 25 mins
- **Ingr.**: 1 grand cauliflower (in steaks), duo tbsp olive essence, tsp paprika, tsp garlic essence, seasoning.
- **Servings**: 4
- **Process**:
    1. Heat at 425°F (220°C).
    2. Adorn steaks with olive essence, dust with spices.
    3. Bake till golden hues appear.
- **Shopping List**: Cauliflower, olive essence, paprika, garlic essence.
- **Tips**: Gentle cutting preserves steak integrity.

Asparagus with Lemon Zest

- **P.T.**: 15 mins
- **Ingr.**: Bunch asparagus (trimmed), duo tbsp olive essence, zest from 1 lemon, seasoning.
- **Servings**: 4
- **Process**:
    1. Oven at 400°F (200°C).
    2. Combine asparagus with olive essence, lemon zest, seasoning.
    3. Oven roast till asparagus softens.
- **Shopping List**: Asparagus, olive essence, lemon.
- **Tips**: Pair with a white fish for complementary flavors.

Brussels in Garlic Aroma

- **P.T.**: 30 mins
- **Ingr.**: 3 cups Brussels sprouts (halved), trio garlic cloves (minced), duo tbsp olive essence, seasoning.

- **Servings**: 4
- **Process**:
  1. Preheat to 375°F (190°C).
  2. Blend sprouts with garlic, olive essence, seasoning.
  3. Roast to achieve crispiness.
- **Shopping List**: Brussels sprouts, garlic, olive essence.
- **Tips**: Dry sprouts pre-roasting for optimal crisp.

Mushroom Ensemble

- **P.T.**: 20 mins
- **Ingr.**: Duo cups fungi (sliced), 1 onion (sliced), duo tbsp balsamic condiment, spoonful of olive essence, thyme, seasoning.
- **Servings**: 4
- **Process**:
  1. Glaze onion in olive essence till softened.
  2. Introduce fungi, cook to brown.
  3. Add balsamic, thyme, seasoning.
- **Shopping List**: Fungi, onion, balsamic condiment, olive essence, thyme.
- **Tips**: Ideal atop grilled meats.

Carrot Ribbons in Citrus Glaze

- **P.T.**: 20 mins
- **Ingr.**: Duo cups carrot (sliced), duo tbsp orange liquid, spoonful of honey, tsp ginger (grated), spoonful of olive essence, seasoning.
- **Servings**: 4
- **Process**:
  1. Lightly sauté carrot in olive essence.
  2. Introduce orange liquid, honey, ginger, seasoning.
  3. Cook to a glaze.
- **Shopping List**: Carrots, orange liquid, honey, ginger, olive essence.
- **Tips**: Honey adjustment for sweetness preference.

Beet Slices in Balsamic Veil

- **P.T.**: 35 mins
- **Ingr.**: Trio beets (sliced), duo tbsp balsamic reduction, spoonful of olive essence, seasoning.
- **Servings**: 4
- **Process**:
  1. Preheat to 375°F (190°C).
  2. Marinate beet slices with olive essence, balsamic, seasoning.
  3. Roast till tender.
- **Shopping List**: Beets, balsamic reduction, olive essence.
- **Tips**: Nest atop greens for a salad variation.

Green Beans with Almond Crunch

- **P.T.**: 15 mins
- **Ingr.**: Duo cups green beans (trimmed), ¼ cup almonds (slivered), spoonful of olive essence, tsp mixed herbs, seasoning.
- **Servings**: 4
- **Process**:
    1. Briefly boil beans, then cool in ice water.
    2. Sauté almonds in olive essence till golden.
    3. Combine beans, herbs, seasoning, sauté briefly.
- **Shopping List**: Green beans, almonds, olive essence, herbs.
- **Tips**: Almond toasting prior to inclusion.

Eggplant Charred with Smokiness

- **P.T.**: 30 mins
- **Ingr.**: Duo eggplants (sliced), duo tbsp olive essence, tsp smoked paprika, seasoning.
- **Servings**: 4
- **Process**:
    1. Brush eggplant slices with olive essence, season with paprika, salt, pepper.
    2. Grill to achieve charring.
- **Shopping List**: Eggplants, olive essence, smoked paprika.
- **Tips**: Salt slices pre-grilling to extract moisture.

Corn Off the Cob in Spice

- **P.T.**: 15 mins
- **Ingr.**: Quartet ears corn (kernels removed), spoonful of olive essence, tsp chili dust, juice from 1 lime, seasoning.
- **Servings**: 4

- **Process**:
    1. Warm olive essence in skillet.
    2. Add corn, chili dust, seasoning, cook to tenderness.
    3. Finish with lime juice.
- **Shopping List**: Corn, olive essence, chili dust, lime.
- **Tips**: Fresh corn kernels yield superior taste and texture.

Squash Cubes

- **P.T.**: 40 mins
- **Ingr.**: 1 butternut squash (cubed), duo tbsp olive essence, tsp cinnamon, seasoning.
- **Servings**: 4
- **Process**:
    1. Combine squash cubes with olive essence, cinnamon, seasoning.
    2. Roast at 400°F (200°C) till tender.
- **Shopping List**: Butternut squash, olive essence, cinnamon.
- **Tips**: Balsamic drizzle adds a sweet-tangy contrast.

Roasted Rainbow Carrots with Herb Drizzle

- **P.T.**: 40 mins
- **Ingr.**:
  - 2 lbs rainbow carrots, trimmed and halved lengthwise
  - 2 tbsp olive oil
  - 1 tbsp mixed fresh herbs (thyme, rosemary, parsley), finely chopped
  - 2 garlic cloves, minced
  - Salt and pepper to taste
- **Servings**: 4
- **Process**:
  1. Toss carrots with olive oil, salt, and pepper.
  2. Roast in a preheated oven at 400°F (200°C) until tender and caramelized, about 30 minutes.
  3. Mix herbs and garlic, sprinkle over roasted carrots.
- **Shopping List**: Rainbow carrots, olive oil, fresh herbs, garlic.
- **Tips**: Great as a colorful side dish. For extra flavor, add a squeeze of lemon juice before serving.

Grilled Zucchini with Lemon and Sea Salt

- **P.T.**: 20 mins
- **Ingr.**:
  - 4 medium zucchinis, sliced lengthwise
  - 2 tbsp olive oil
  - 1 lemon, zest and juice
  - Sea salt and cracked black pepper
- **Servings**: 4
- **Process**:
  1. Brush zucchini slices with olive oil, season with salt and pepper.
  2. Grill over medium heat until tender and grill marks appear, about 3-4 minutes per side.
  3. Drizzle with lemon juice and sprinkle lemon zest.
- **Shopping List**: Zucchinis, olive oil, lemon.
- **Tips**: Serve warm as a light and refreshing side dish. Can be paired with any grilled protein.

Spiced Cauliflower Steaks

- **P.T.**: 30 mins
- **Ingr.**:
  - 1 large cauliflower, sliced into 1/2 inch thick steaks
  - 2 tbsp olive oil
  - 1 tsp smoked paprika
  - 1/2 tsp ground cumin
  - 1/4 tsp cayenne pepper (optional)
  - Salt and pepper to taste

- **Servings**: 4
- **Process**:
  1. Brush cauliflower steaks with olive oil.
  2. Mix paprika, cumin, cayenne, salt, and pepper, sprinkle over cauliflower.
  3. Roast at 400°F (200°C) until tender and golden, about 20 minutes.

- **Shopping List**: Cauliflower, olive oil, smoked paprika, ground cumin, cayenne pepper.
- **Tips**: Cauliflower steaks can be served as a main course for a vegetarian meal or as a unique side dish.

Chapter 7: Recipes with Red Meat

Herb-Infused Bovine Sauté

- **P.T.**: 25 mins
- **Ingr.**: 1 lb bovine sirloin (sliced), 1 tbsp rosemary (chopped), 1 tbsp thyme (chopped), 2 tbsp olive essence, 2 garlic cloves (minced), sea salt, pepper.
- **Servings**: 4
- **Process**:

1. Heat olive essence in a pan on medium flame.
2. Sauté bovine slices with garlic, rosemary, thyme, seasoning.
3. Cook until preferred tenderness.

- **Shopping List**: Bovine sirloin, rosemary, thyme, olive essence, garlic.
- **Tips**: Resting the meat post-cooking ensures juiciness.

Lamb Skewers, Eastern Spiced

- **P.T.**: 35 mins (includes marination)
- **Ingr.**: 1 lb lamb shoulder (cubed), 2 tbsp olive essence, 1 tsp cumin, 1 tsp paprika, 1 tsp garlic essence, seasoning, wooden skewers.
- **Servings**: 4
- **Process**:
  1. Marinate lamb in olive essence, cumin, paprika, garlic essence, seasoning for 30 mins.
  2. Thread lamb onto skewers.
  3. Grill on medium flame till cooked.
- **Shopping List**: Lamb shoulder, olive essence, cumin, paprika, garlic essence, skewers.
- **Tips**: Soaking skewers prevents charring.

Rosemary & Garlic Bovine Roast

- **P.T.**: 1 hr 30 mins
- **Ingr.**: 2 lb bovine roast, 3 tbsp rosemary (chopped), 4 garlic cloves (minced), 2 tbsp olive essence, sea salt, pepper.
- **Servings**: 6
- **Process**:
  1. Oven at 350°F (175°C).
  2. Rub roast with olive essence, garlic, rosemary, seasoning.
  3. Roast until desired doneness.
- **Shopping List**: Bovine roast, rosemary, garlic, olive essence.
- **Tips**: Meat thermometer for precise cooking.

Flank Steak with Chimichurri

- **P.T.:** 30 mins
- **Ingr.:** 1 lb flank steak, for chimichurri: 1 cup parsley, 3 garlic cloves, ½ cup olive essence, 2 tbsp vinegar, 1 tsp red pepper flakes, seasoning.

- **Servings**: 4
- **Process**:
  1. Grill flank steak to preferred doneness.
  2. Blend parsley, garlic, olive essence, vinegar, red pepper flakes, seasoning for sauce.
  3. Serve steak with chimichurri.
- **Shopping List**: Flank steak, parsley, garlic, olive essence, vinegar, red pepper flakes.
- **Tips**: Rest steak, slice against grain.

Short Ribs in Balsamic Glaze

- **P.T.:** 2 hrs 30 mins
- **Ingr.:** 2 lbs beef short ribs, 1 cup balsamic reduction, 2 tbsp olive essence, 2 garlic cloves (minced), seasoning.
- **Servings**: 4
- **Process**:
    1. Sear ribs with garlic, olive essence, seasoning.
    2. Add balsamic, simmer on low flame till tender.
- **Shopping List**: Beef short ribs, balsamic reduction, olive essence, garlic.
- **Tips**: Slow simmer for tenderness.

Lemon & Herb Lamb Riblets

- **P.T.:** 20 mins
- **Ingr.:** 1 lb lamb chops, 2 tbsp lemon liquid, 1 tbsp rosemary (chopped), 1 tbsp thyme (chopped), 2 tbsp olive essence, seasoning.
- **Servings**: 4
- **Process**:
    1. Marinate lamb in lemon liquid, rosemary, thyme, olive essence, seasoning for 15 mins.
    2. Grill on medium flame.
- **Shopping List**: Lamb chops, lemon liquid, rosemary, thyme, olive essence.
- **Tips**: Avoid overcrowding grill for even cooking.

Savory Ground Bovine Orbs

- **P.T.**: 40 mins
- **Ingr.**: 1 lb ground bovine, 1 cup tomato concoction, 1 onion (minced), 1 garlic clove (minced), 1 egg, 2 tbsp parsley (chopped), seasoning.
- **Servings**: 4
- **Process**:

1. Combine ground bovine, onion, garlic, egg, parsley, seasoning.
2. Form into orbs, brown in skillet.
3. Introduce tomato concoction, simmer till cooked.

- **Shopping List**: Ground bovine, tomato concoction, onion, garlic, egg, parsley.
- **Tips**: Damp hands prevent sticking when forming orbs.

Bovine Stroganoff with Tropical Cream

- **P.T.**: 35 mins
- **Ingr.**: 1 lb bovine strips, 1 onion (sliced), 1 cup fungi (sliced), 1 cup coconut cream, 2 tbsp olive essence, seasoning.
- **Servings**: 4
- **Process**:
  1. Sauté bovine strips in olive essence, set aside.
  2. Cook onion, fungi, seasoning.
  3. Introduce bovine, add coconut cream, simmer.
- **Shopping List**: Bovine strips, onion, fungi, coconut cream, olive essence.
- **Tips**: Full-fat coconut cream for richness.

Bovine and Veg Stir-Fry

- **P.T.**: 30 mins
- **Ingr.**: 1 lb bovine sirloin (sliced), 2 cups mixed vegetables, 2 tbsp soy condiment, 1 tbsp ginger (grated), 1 tsp chili flakes, 2 tbsp olive essence.
- **Servings**: 4
- **Process**:
  1. Stir-fry bovine in olive essence, reserve.
  2. Cook vegetables, ginger, chili.
  3. Introduce bovine back, toss with soy condiment.
- **Shopping List**: Bovine sirloin, mixed vegetables, soy condiment, ginger, chili flakes, olive essence.
- **Tips**: Thin bovine slices for quick stir-fry.

Slow-Braised Bovine Brisket

- **P.T.**: 3 hrs
- **Ingr.**: 2 lbs bovine brisket, 1 onion (chopped), 2 carrots (chopped), 2 celery stalks (chopped), 4 cups bovine broth, 2 tbsp olive essence, thyme, bay leaves, seasoning.
- **Servings**: 6

- **Process**:
    1. Brown brisket in olive essence.
    2. Add vegetables, thyme, bay leaves, seasoning.
    3. Cover with broth, simmer on low flame till tender.
- **Shopping List**: Bovine brisket, onion, carrots, celery, bovine broth, olive essence, thyme, bay leaves.
- **Tips**: Lengthy cooking develops rich flavors.

Moroccan-Spiced Beef Tagine

- **P.T.**: 1 hour 30 mins
- **Ingr.**:
  - 2 lbs beef stew meat, cubed
  - 1 onion, chopped
  - 2 carrots, sliced
  - 1 can diced tomatoes
  - 2 cups beef broth
  - 2 tsp ground cumin
  - 1 tsp ground cinnamon
  - 1 tsp paprika
  - 2 tbsp olive oil
  - Salt and pepper to taste
- **Servings**: 4
- **Process**:

1. Brown beef in olive oil, set aside.
2. Sauté onions and carrots until softened.
3. Add spices, then beef, tomatoes, and broth.
4. Simmer covered for 1 hour or until meat is tender.

- **Shopping List**: Beef stew meat, onion, carrots, canned tomatoes, beef broth, cumin, cinnamon, paprika, olive oil.
- **Tips**: Serve with couscous or flatbread. Garnish with fresh cilantro for extra flavor.

Grilled Steak with Chimichurri Sauce

- **P.T.**: 25 mins
- **Ingr.**:
  - 2 ribeye steaks
  - 1/2 cup fresh parsley
  - 1/4 cup fresh cilantro
  - 3 garlic cloves
  - 1/2 cup olive oil
  - 2 tbsp red wine vinegar
  - 1/2 tsp red pepper flakes
  - Salt and pepper to taste
- **Servings**: 2
- **Process**:

1. Season steaks with salt and pepper, grill to desired doneness.
2. Blend parsley, cilantro, garlic, olive oil, vinegar, red pepper flakes for chimichurri.
3. Serve steak with chimichurri sauce.

- **Shopping List**: Ribeye steaks, parsley, cilantro, garlic, olive oil, red wine vinegar, red pepper flakes.

- **Tips**: Let steaks rest for a few minutes after grilling before serving.

Rosemary Balsamic Braised Lamb Shanks

- **P.T.**: 2 hours 30 mins
- **Ingr.**:
  - 4 lamb shanks
  - 1 onion, chopped
  - 2 cups beef broth
  - 1 cup balsamic vinegar
  - 4 rosemary sprigs
  - 3 garlic cloves, minced
  - 2 tbsp olive oil
  - Salt and pepper to taste
- **Servings**: 4
- **Process**:
  1. Season lamb with salt and pepper, brown in olive oil.
  2. Remove lamb, sauté onion and garlic.
  3. Add vinegar, broth, rosemary, return lamb to pot.
  4. Cover and braise in the oven at 325°F (160°C) for 2 hours.

- **Shopping List**: Lamb shanks, onion, beef broth, balsamic vinegar, rosemary, garlic, olive oil.

- **Tips**: Serve with mashed potatoes or polenta for a hearty meal.

Chapter 8: Pork Recipes

Citrus-Infused Porcine Filet

- **P.T.**: 45 mins
- **Ingr.**: 1 porcine tenderloin (approx. 1 lb), 2 tbsp citrus juice, 1 tbsp zested lemon, 1 tbsp rosemary (chopped), 1 tbsp thyme (chopped), 2 tbsp olive essence, sea salt, cracked pepper.
- **Servings**: 4
- **Process**:
    1. Marinate porcine in citrus blend, rosemary, thyme, olive essence, seasoning for 30 mins.
    2. Oven-roast at 375°F (190°C) until perfectly cooked.
- **Shopping List**: Porcine tenderloin, citrus juice, lemon, rosemary, thyme, olive essence.
- **Tips**: Rest porcine post-roasting for succulent slices.

Spicy Swine Belly

- **P.T.**: 2 hrs
- **Ingr.**: 1 lb swine belly, 1 tsp cumin, 1 tsp paprika, 1 tsp garlic essence, 2 tbsp olive essence, seasoning.
- **Servings**: 4
- **Process**:
    1. Coat swine belly with olive essence, cumin, paprika, garlic essence, seasoning.
    2. Slow-roast at 325°F (163°C) for crisp exterior, tender core.
- **Shopping List**: Swine belly, cumin, paprika, garlic essence, olive essence.
- **Tips**: Scoring skin enhances crackling texture.

Grilled Pork Loin with Orchard Salsa

- **P.T.**: 30 mins
- **Ingr.**: 4 pork loin cuts, 1 orchard fruit (diced), 1 red bulb (diced), 2 tbsp citrus juice, 1 tbsp cilantro (chopped), seasoning.
- **Servings**: 4
- **Process**:
  1. Grill pork loin to perfection.
  2. Mix orchard fruit, red bulb, citrus juice, cilantro for salsa.
  3. Top loin with orchard salsa.
- **Shopping List**: Pork loin, orchard fruit, red bulb, citrus juice, cilantro.
- **Tips**: Rest loin after grilling for enhanced tenderness.

Slow Simmered Swine Shoulder

- **P.T.**: 8 hrs (slow cooker)
- **Ingr.**: 2 lb swine shoulder, 1 bulb (sliced), 4 garlic cloves (minced), 1 cup poultry broth, 2 tbsp apple cider vinegar, 1 tbsp smoked paprika, olive essence, salt, pepper.
- **Servings**: 6
- **Process**:
  1. Sear swine in olive essence.
  2. Place sliced bulb, garlic in cooker, top with swine.
  3. Add broth, vinegar, paprika, seasoning.
  4. Slow cook till tender.
- **Shopping List**: Swine shoulder, bulb, garlic, poultry broth, apple cider vinegar, smoked paprika, olive essence.
- **Tips**: Shred for a pulled-style dish.

Pork and Veggie Wok Toss

P.T.: 25 mins

- **Ingr.**: 1 lb pork fillet (sliced), 2 cups mixed greens, 2 tbsp soy elixir, 1 tbsp ginger (grated), 2 tbsp olive essence, salt, pepper.
- **Servings**: 4
- **Process**:
    1. Wok fry pork in olive essence until bronzed.
    2. Add greens, ginger, seasoning.
    3. Drizzle with soy elixir, wok toss until greens tenderize.
- **Shopping List**: Pork fillet, mixed greens, soy elixir, ginger, olive essence.
- **Tips**: Thin pork slices expedite cooking.

Herbed Swine Ribs

- **P.T.**: 1 hr 20 mins
- **Ingr.**: 2 lbs swine ribs, 1 tbsp rosemary (chopped), 1 tbsp thyme (chopped), 2 tbsp olive essence, sea salt, pepper.
- **Servings**: 4
- **Process**:
    1. Infuse ribs with olive essence, rosemary, thyme, seasoning.
    2. Oven-bake at 350°F (175°C) till tenderness achieved.
- **Shopping List**: Swine ribs, rosemary, thyme, olive essence.
- **Tips**: Cover ribs initially with foil to retain moisture.

Roasted Loin of Pork with Root Veggies

- **P.T.**: 1 hr
- **Ingr.**: 1 pork loin (about 2 lbs), duo carrots (chopped), duo parsnips (chopped), 1 bulb (chopped), 2 tbsp olive essence, 1 tbsp garlic essence, seasoning.
- **Servings**: 6
- **Process**:
    1. Adorn loin with olive essence, garlic essence, seasoning.
    2. Surround with carrots, parsnips, bulb.
    3. Roast at 375°F (190°C) till pork cooks thoroughly.
- **Shopping List**: Pork loin, carrots, parsnips, bulb, olive essence, garlic essence.
- **Tips**: Thermometer ensures accurate doneness.

Smoked Pulled Pork

- **P.T.**: 8 hrs (slow cooker)
- **Ingr.**: 3 lbs pork butt, 1 tbsp smoked paprika, 1 tbsp garlic essence, 2 tbsp apple cider vinegar, 1 cup poultry broth, olive essence, seasoning.
- **Servings**: 8
- **Process**:
    1. Blend paprika, garlic essence, seasoning, rub on pork.
    2. Sear in olive essence.
    3. Place in cooker with vinegar, broth.
    4. Slow cook for pull-apart tenderness.
- **Shopping List**: Pork butt, smoked paprika, garlic essence, apple cider vinegar, poultry broth, olive essence.
- **Tips**: Serve shredded with barbeque sauce.

Garlic and Citrus Marinated Pork Filet

- **P.T.:** 1 hr (includes marination)
- **Ingr.:** 1 pork filet (about 1 lb), 4 garlic cloves (minced), juice of 2 citrus fruits, 2 tbsp olive essence, seasoning.
- **Servings:** 4

- **Process:**
    1. Marinate pork in garlic, citrus juice, olive essence, seasoning for 30 mins.
    2. Grill or oven-roast until cooked through.
- **Shopping List:** Pork filet, garlic, citrus fruits, olive essence.
- **Tips:** Rest meat before slicing.

Spicy Pork and Capsicum Sauté

- **P.T.:** 30 mins
- **Ingr.:** 1 lb pork fillet (sliced), duo bell capsicums (sliced), 1 bulb (sliced), tsp chili flakes, 2 tbsp olive essence, seasoning.
- **Servings:** 4
- **Process:**
    1. Sauté pork in olive essence, remove.
    2. Introduce capsicums, bulb, chili flakes, seasoning.
    3. Return pork, cook till capsicums soften.
- **Shopping List:** Pork fillet, bell capsicums, bulb, chili flakes, olive essence.
- **Tips:** Adjust chili for desired spiciness.

Herbed Pork Tenderloin with Apple Cider Reduction

- **P.T.**: 45 mins
- **Ingr.**:
  - 2 pork tenderloins (about 1 lb each)
  - 2 cups apple cider
  - 2 tbsp fresh rosemary, minced
  - 2 tbsp fresh thyme, minced
  - 2 garlic cloves, minced
  - 2 tbsp olive oil
  - Salt and pepper to taste
- **Servings**: 4
- **Process**:
  1. Rub tenderloins with garlic, rosemary, thyme, salt, and pepper.
  2. In a skillet, sear tenderloins in olive oil until browned.
  3. Remove pork, add apple cider to deglaze the pan.
  1. Simmer cider until reduced by half and pour over pork.
- **Shopping List**: Pork tenderloins, apple cider, rosemary, thyme, garlic, olive oil.
- **Tips**: Let the pork rest for a few minutes before slicing. Serve with roasted vegetables.

Spiced Pork Ribs with Smoky BBQ Glaze

- **P.T.**: 1 hour 30 mins
- **Ingr.**:
  - 2 racks pork ribs
  - 1/4 cup paprika
  - 1 tbsp smoked paprika
  - 1 tbsp garlic powder
  - 1 tbsp onion powder
  - 1/2 tbsp cayenne pepper
  - 1/2 cup BBQ sauce (Whole30 compliant)
  - 2 tbsp honey (optional)
  - Salt and pepper to taste
- **Servings**: 4-6
- **Process**:
  1. Mix paprikas, garlic and onion powder, cayenne, salt, and pepper.
  2. Rub spice mix over ribs.
  3. Grill ribs over indirect heat, covered, for 1 hour.

4. Glaze with BBQ sauce (and honey if using), grill for additional 15 mins.

- **Shopping List**: Pork ribs, paprikas, garlic powder, onion powder, cayenne pepper, BBQ sauce, honey.

- **Tips**: For a deeper flavor, allow the ribs to marinate with the spice rub overnight.

Pork Loin Roast with Fennel and Herbs

- **P.T.**: 2 hours
- **Ingr.**:
  - 3 lb pork loin roast
  - 2 fennel bulbs, sliced
  - 1 onion, sliced
  - 4 garlic cloves, minced
  - 2 tbsp fresh sage, chopped
  - 2 tbsp fresh rosemary, chopped
  - 2 tbsp olive oil
  - Salt and pepper to taste
- **Servings**: 6

- **Process**:
  1. Preheat oven to 350°F (175°C).
  2. Season pork loin with salt, pepper, garlic, sage, and rosemary.
  3. In a roasting pan, layer fennel and onion, place pork on top.
  4. Roast for 1.5 to 2 hours or until internal temperature reaches 145°F (63°C).

- **Shopping List**: Pork loin roast, fennel bulbs, onion, garlic, sage, rosemary, olive oil.
- **Tips**: Let the roast rest for 10 minutes before slicing. The fennel and onion make a delicious side.

Chapter 9: Poultry Preparation

Aromatic Fowl Roast

- **P.T.:** 1 hr 20 mins
- **Ingr.:** 1 whole fowl (approx. 4 lbs), 4 cloves garlic (minced), 2 tbsp rosemary (chopped), 2 tbsp thyme (chopped), 2 tbsp olive essence, sea salt, cracked pepper.
- **Servings**: 4-6
- **Process**:

1. Oven preheat to 375°F (190°C).
2. Blend garlic, rosemary, thyme, olive essence, seasoning, massage onto fowl.
3. Roast until internal temp reaches 165°F (74°C).

- **Shopping List**: Whole fowl, garlic, rosemary, thyme, olive essence.
- **Tips**: Resting the fowl post-roast ensures moist meat.

Fiery Fowl Stir-Toss

- **P.T.**: 30 mins
- **Ingr.**: 1 lb fowl breast (sliced), 2 cups varied veggies, 2 tbsp soy elixir, 1 tbsp ginger (grated), 1 tsp chili shards, 2 tbsp olive essence.
- **Servings**: 4
- **Process**:
    1. Olive essence stir-fry of fowl until bronzed.
    2. Toss in veggies, ginger, chili shards, seasoning.
    3. Finish with soy elixir, stir until veggies tender.
- **Shopping List**: Fowl breast, varied veggies, soy elixir, ginger, chili shards, olive essence.
- **Tips**: Thin slices of fowl ensure swift cooking.

Citrus-Thyme Fowl Skillet

- **P.T.**: 35 mins
- **Ingr.**: 4 fowl thighs, 2 citrus (sliced), 1 tbsp thyme (chopped), 2 tbsp olive essence, seasoning.
- **Servings**: 4
- **Process**:
    1. Golden sauté of fowl in olive essence.
    2. Introduce citrus slices, thyme, cook till fowl is done.
- **Shopping List**: Fowl thighs, citrus, thyme, olive essence.
- **Tips**: A splash of broth can enhance the skillet flavors.

Avocado-Topped Grilled Fowl

- **P.T.**: 45 mins
- **Ingr.**: 4 fowl breasts, 1 avocado (cubed), 1 tomato (cubed), 1 lime (juice), 1 tbsp cilantro (chopped), 2 tbsp olive essence, seasoning.
- **Servings**: 4
- **Process**:
    1. Grill fowl till cooked through.
    2. Mix avocado, tomato, lime juice, cilantro for salsa.
    3. Adorn grilled fowl with avocado salsa.
- **Shopping List**: Fowl breasts, avocado, tomato, lime, cilantro, olive essence.
- **Tips**: Rest fowl before salsa topping.

Sage & Rosemary Turkey Fillet

- **P.T.**: 1 hr
- **Ingr.**: 1 turkey breast (approx. 3 lbs), 2 tbsp sage (chopped), 2 tbsp rosemary (chopped), 2 tbsp olive essence, seasoning.
- **Servings**: 4-6
- **Process**:
    1. Oven at 350°F (175°C).
    2. Rub turkey with olive essence, sage, rosemary, seasoning.
    3. Roast till internal temp reaches 165°F (74°C).
- **Shopping List**: Turkey breast, sage, rosemary, olive essence.
- **Tips**: Baste periodically for moisture.

Fowl and Greens on Skewers

- **P.T.:** 40 mins (includes marinating)
- **Ingr.:** 1 lb fowl breast (cubed), greens (bell peppers, onions, zucchini), 2 tbsp olive essence, 1 tbsp garlic essence, seasoning, skewers.

- **Servings**: 4
- **Process**:
  1. Marinate fowl in olive essence, garlic essence, seasoning for 30 mins.
  2. Skewer fowl and greens.
  3. Grill until fowl is cooked.
- **Shopping List**: Fowl breast, greens, olive essence, garlic essence, skewers.
- **Tips**: Soak wooden skewers to prevent burning.

Tagine of Moroccan Fowl

- **P.T.:** 1 hr
- **Ingr.:** 4 fowl thighs, 1 bulb (chopped), 2 garlic cloves (minced), 1 tsp cumin, 1 tsp paprika, 1 cup poultry broth, 2 tbsp olive essence, seasoning.
- **Servings**: 4
- **Process**:
  1. Brown fowl in olive essence.

  2. Add bulb, garlic, spices, cook shortly.
  3. Pour in broth, simmer till fowl softens.
- **Shopping List**: Fowl thighs, bulb, garlic, cumin, paprika, poultry broth, olive essence.
- **Tips**: Couscous makes an ideal accompaniment.

Baked Fowl with Olive and Tomato

- **P.T.**: 50 mins
- **Ingr.**: 4 fowl breasts, 1 cup olives, 1 cup cherry tomatoes, 2 tbsp olive essence, 1 tbsp oregano, seasoning.
- **Servings**: 4
- **Process**:
  1. Arrange fowl in baking dish.
  2. Scatter olives, tomatoes, drizzle olive essence, oregano, seasoning.
  3. Oven-bake till fowl is cooked.
- **Shopping List**: Fowl breasts, olives, cherry tomatoes, olive essence, oregano.
- **Tips**: White wine adds a flavor boost.

Asian Fowl Lettuce Cups

- **P.T.**: 25 mins
- **Ingr.**: 1 lb ground fowl, 1 lettuce head, 1 bulb (diced), 2 tbsp soy elixir, 1 tbsp sesame essence, 1 tsp ginger (grated), seasoning.
- **Servings**: 4
- **Process**:
  1. Cook ground fowl with bulb, ginger, seasoning.
  2. Stir in soy elixir, sesame essence.
  3. Serve in lettuce leaves.
- **Shopping List**: Ground fowl, lettuce, bulb, soy elixir, sesame essence, ginger.
- **Tips**: Water chestnuts add a crunchy texture.

Paprika-Infused Fowl Thighs

- **P.T.**: 40 mins
- **Ingr.**: 4 fowl thighs, 2 tbsp smoked paprika, 1 tbsp garlic essence, 2 tbsp olive essence, seasoning.
- **Servings**: 4
- **Process**:
    1. Coat fowl with olive essence, smoked paprika, garlic essence, seasoning.
    2. Oven-bake at 375°F (190°C) until done.
- **Shopping List**: Fowl thighs, smoked paprika, garlic essence, olive essence.
- **Tips**: Rest fowl to ensure moisture retention.

Lemon and Thyme Roast Chicken

- **P.T.**: 1 hour 20 mins
- **Ingr.**:
    - 1 whole chicken (about 4 lbs)
    - 2 lemons, one sliced and one juiced
    - 4 sprigs fresh thyme
    - 3 garlic cloves, minced
    - 2 tbsp olive oil
    - Salt and pepper to taste
- **Servings**: 4-6
- **Process**:
    1. Preheat oven to 375°F (190°C).
    2. Rub the chicken with olive oil, lemon juice, garlic, salt, and pepper.
    3. Stuff the cavity with lemon slices and thyme sprigs.
    4. Roast for 1 hour or until the internal temperature reaches 165°F (74°C).
- **Shopping List**: Whole chicken, lemons, thyme, garlic, olive oil.
- **Tips**: Let the chicken rest for 10 minutes before carving. Serve with roast vegetables.

Spiced Chicken Skewers with Yogurt Dip

- **P.T.**: 45 mins
- **Ingr.**:
  - 2 lbs chicken breast, cut into cubes
  - 2 tsp paprika
  - 1 tsp cumin
  - 1/2 tsp cayenne pepper
  - 1 cup Greek yogurt
  - 2 tbsp mint, chopped
  - 2 tbsp olive oil
  - Salt and pepper to taste
- **Servings**: 4
- **Process**:
  1. Marinate chicken cubes in olive oil, paprika, cumin, cayenne, salt, and pepper.
  2. Thread chicken onto skewers.
  3. Grill over medium heat until cooked through.
  4. Mix yogurt with mint for dipping.
- **Shopping List**: Chicken breast, paprika, cumin, cayenne pepper, Greek yogurt, mint, olive oil.
- **Tips**: If using wooden skewers, soak in water for 30 minutes before use to prevent burning.

Balsamic Glazed Turkey Meatballs

- **P.T.**: 35 mins
- **Ingr.**:
  - 1 lb ground turkey
  - 1/2 cup breadcrumbs
  - 1 egg
  - 3 tbsp balsamic vinegar
  - 2 tbsp honey
  - 1 garlic clove, minced
  - 2 tbsp olive oil
  - Salt and pepper to taste
- **Servings**: 4
- **Process**:
  1. Combine ground turkey, breadcrumbs, egg, garlic, salt, and pepper.
  2. Form into meatballs.

3. Brown meatballs in olive oil, then add balsamic vinegar and honey.

4. Simmer until glaze is reduced.

- **Shopping List**: Ground turkey, breadcrumbs, egg, balsamic vinegar, honey, garlic, olive oil.

- **Tips**: Serve with a side of steamed vegetables or over whole grain pasta.

Chapter 10: Fish and Seafood

Cod in Mediterranean Essence

- **P.T.**: 30 mins
- **Ingr.**: Quartet cod slabs, 1 cup cherry tomatos (halved), 1 citrus (sliced), 2 tbsp olive essence, 1 tbsp oregano, sea salt, cracked pepper.
- **Servings**: 4
- **Process**:

1. Position cod in baking vessel, encircle with tomatos, citrus slices.
2. Drizzle olive essence, scatter oregano, seasoning.
3. Oven at 375°F (190°C) until cod flakey.

- **Shopping List**: Cod slabs, cherry tomatos, citrus, olive essence, oregano.
- **Tips**: Serve alongside quinoa for wholesome meal.

Ginger Soy Glazed Salmon

- **P.T.:** 25 mins
- **Ingr.:** Quartet salmon fillets, 2 tbsp soy elixir, 1 tbsp ginger (grated), 1 tbsp honey, 2 tbsp olive essence.
- **Servings**: 4
- **Process**:
    1. Marinade salmon in soy elixir, ginger, honey, olive essence for 15 mins.
    2. Grill or pan-sear till done.
- **Shopping List**: Salmon fillets, soy elixir, ginger, honey, olive essence.
- **Tips**: Avoid excess cooking; salmon should be slightly rosy within.

Fiery Shrimp with Garlic

P.T.: 20 mins
- **Ingr.:** 1 lb shrimp (peeled, deveined), 3 garlic cloves (minced), 1 tsp chili shards, 2 tbsp olive essence, sea salt, pepper.
- **Servings**: 4
- **Process**:
    1. Olive essence sauté of garlic and chili shards.
    2. Add shrimp, cook till pink and opaque.
- **Shopping List**: Shrimp, garlic, chili shards, olive essence.
- **Tips**: Pair with cauliflower rice for a low-carb dish.

Citrus-Dill Trout Bake

- **P.T.**: 25 mins
- **Ingr.**: Quartet trout fillets, 2 citrus (sliced), 2 tbsp dill (chopped), 2 tbsp olive essence, sea salt, pepper.
- **Servings**: 4

- **Process**:
  1. Arrange trout in baking dish, top with citrus, dill.
  2. Drizzle olive essence, season.
  3. Bake at 350°F (175°C) till flaky.
- **Shopping List**: Trout fillets, citrus, dill, olive essence.
- **Tips**: Complement with steamed green veggies.

Seared Tuna with Avocado Mix

- **P.T.**: 30 mins
- **Ingr.**: Quartet tuna steaks, 1 avocado (cubed), 1 tomato (cubed), 1 lime (juice), 1 tbsp cilantro (chopped), 2 tbsp olive essence, sea salt, pepper.
- **Servings**: 4
- **Process**:
  1. Sear tuna steaks to desired level.
  2. Combine avocado, tomato, lime juice, cilantro for salsa.
  3. Serve tuna with salsa topping.
- **Shopping List**: Tuna steaks, avocado, tomato, lime, cilantro, olive essence.
- **Tips**: Tuna best slightly pink at center.

Scallops in Garlic-Butter

- **P.T.**: 20 mins
- **Ingr.**: 1 lb scallops, 4 tbsp butter, 2 garlic cloves (minced), seasoning.
- **Servings**: 4
- **Process**:
    1. Sear scallops in butter and garlic mix until golden.
    2. Season with salt and pepper.
- **Shopping List**: Scallops, butter, garlic.
- **Tips**: Dry scallops before searing for golden crust.

Herb-Coated Halibut

- **P.T.**: 30 mins
- **Ingr.**: Quartet halibut fillets, 2 tbsp parsley (chopped), 2 tbsp basil (chopped), 2 tbsp olive essence, seasoning.
- **Servings**: 4
- **Process**:
    1. Coat halibut with olive essence, herbs, seasoning.
    2. Bake at 375°F (190°C) till done.
- **Shopping List**: Halibut fillets, parsley, basil, olive essence.
- **Tips**: Serve with fresh salad for light meal.

Mussels in Smoked Tomato Broth

- **P.T.**: 25 mins
- **Ingr.**: 2 lbs mussels (cleaned), 1 cup tomato sauce, 1 onion (diced), 2 garlic cloves (minced), 1 tsp smoked paprika, 2 tbsp olive essence, seasoning.
- **Servings**: 4
- **Process**:
    1. Sauté onion, garlic in olive essence.
    2. Introduce tomato sauce, smoked paprika, seasoning, simmer.
    3. Add mussels, cover, cook till they open.
- **Shopping List**: Mussels, tomato sauce, onion, garlic, smoked paprika, olive essence.
- **Tips**: Discard non-opening mussels.

Cajun-Infused Catfish

P.T.: 20 mins
- **Ingr.**: Quartet catfish fillets, 2 tbsp Cajun spice, 2 tbsp olive essence.
- **Servings**: 4
- **Process**:
    1. Rub catfish with Cajun spice.
    2. Pan-fry in olive essence till cooked.
- **Shopping List**: Catfish fillets, Cajun spice, olive essence.
- **Tips**: Accompany with sautéed greens.

Pesto Crusted Salmon Bake

- **P.T.**: 30 mins
- **Ingr.**: Quartet salmon fillets, 4 tbsp pesto, 2 tbsp olive essence, seasoning.
- **Servings**: 4

- **Process**:
    1. Spread pesto over salmon fillets.
    2. Drizzle olive essence, season.
    3. Oven at 375°F (190°C) till flaky.
- **Shopping List**: Salmon fillets, pesto, olive essence.
- **Tips**: Serve with roasted veggies for hearty meal.

Garlic-Lime Shrimp Skewers

- **P.T.**: 30 mins
- **Ingr.**:
    - 1 lb large shrimp, peeled and deveined
    - 3 garlic cloves, minced
    - Juice of 2 limes
    - 2 tbsp olive oil
    - 1 tsp chili flakes (optional)
    - Salt and pepper to taste
- **Servings**: 4
- **Process**:

1. Marinate shrimp in garlic, lime juice, olive oil, chili flakes, salt, and pepper for 20 minutes.
2. Thread shrimp onto skewers.
3. Grill over medium heat until opaque, about 3 minutes per side.
- **Shopping List**: Shrimp, garlic, limes, olive oil, chili flakes.

- **Tips**: Serve with a fresh green salad or over a bed of cauliflower rice for a complete meal.

Cod with Olives and Capers

- **P.T.**: 40 mins
- **Ingr.**:
    - 4 cod fillets
    - 1 cup cherry tomatoes, halved
    - 1/2 cup Kalamata olives, pitted
    - 2 tbsp capers
    - 1/4 cup white wine
    - 2 tbsp olive oil
    - 1 garlic clove, minced
    - Salt and pepper to taste
- **Servings**: 4
- **Process**:
    1. Preheat oven to 375°F (190°C).
    2. Place cod in a baking dish, surround with tomatoes, olives, and capers.
    3. Mix white wine, olive oil, and garlic, pour over cod.
    4. Bake for 25 minutes or until fish flakes easily.
- **Shopping List**: Cod fillets, cherry tomatoes, Kalamata olives, capers, white wine, olive oil, garlic.
- **Tips**: This dish pairs well with quinoa or a light pasta.

Asian-Style Steamed Salmon with Ginger and Green Onion

- **P.T.**: 25 mins
- **Ingr.**:
  - 4 salmon fillets
  - 2-inch piece ginger, julienned
  - 4 green onions, thinly sliced
  - 3 tbsp soy sauce (or coconut aminos)
  - 1 tbsp sesame oil
  - 1 tbsp honey (optional)
  - Sesame seeds for garnish
- **Servings**: 4
- **Process**:
  1. Place salmon in a steamer over boiling water.
  2. Top salmon with ginger and green onions.
  3. Steam for 15 minutes or until cooked through.
  4. Combine soy sauce, sesame oil, and honey, drizzle over salmon.
- **Shopping List**: Salmon fillets, ginger, green onions, soy sauce or coconut aminos, sesame oil, honey, sesame seeds.
- **Tips**: Garnish with sesame seeds and serve with steamed vegetables for a balanced meal.

Chapter 11: Healthy Sauces and Condiments

Basil Pesto Fusion

- **P.T.**: 10 mins
- **Ingr.**: Duo cups fresh basil leaves, 1/2 cup pine kernels, 1/2 cup olive essence, trio garlic cloves, salt, cracked pepper.
- **Servings**: 1 cup
- **Process**:
    1. Puree basil, pine kernels, garlic.
    2. Gradually add olive essence during blending.
    3. Season with salt and pepper.
- **Shopping List**: Fresh basil, pine kernels, olive essence, garlic.
- **Tips**: Refrigerate in airtight container to preserve freshness.

Avocado Velouté

- **P.T.**: 15 mins
- **Ingr.**: Duo ripe avocados, juice of 1 citrus, 1/4 cup cilantro, duo tbsp olive essence, salt, pepper.
- **Servings**: 1 cup
- **Process**:
    1. Blend avocados, citrus juice, cilantro, olive essence until creamy.
    2. Add salt and pepper for taste.
- **Shopping List**: Avocados, citrus, cilantro, olive essence.
- **Tips**: Ideal as a dip or a creamy topping.

Tomato and Herb Coulis

- **P.T.**: 30 mins
- **Ingr.**: 1 can crushed tomatoes, 1 bulb (diced), duo garlic cloves (minced), 1/4 cup basil (chopped), duo tbsp olive essence, salt, pepper.
- **Servings**: 2 cups

- **Process**:
    1. Olive essence sauté of bulb and garlic.
    2. Add tomatoes, simmer for 20 mins.
    3. Stir in basil, season with salt and pepper.
- **Shopping List**: Crushed tomatoes, bulb, garlic, basil, olive essence.
- **Tips**: Excellent base for pasta or pizza dishes.

Cilantro-Lime Vinaigrette

- **P.T.**: 10 mins
- **Ingr.**: 1 cup cilantro, juice of 1 lime, 1/2 cup olive essence, 1 garlic clove, salt, pepper.
- **Servings**: 1 cup
- **Process**:
    1. Blend cilantro, lime juice, garlic, and olive essence.
    2. Season with salt and pepper.
- **Shopping List**: Cilantro, lime, olive essence, garlic.
- **Tips**: A versatile dressing or marinade.

Fiery Chipotle Spread

- **P.T.**: 15 mins
- **Ingr.**: 1 cup compliant mayo, duo chipotle chilis in adobo, juice of 1 lime, salt.
- **Servings**: 1 cup
- **Process**:
    1. Blend mayo, chipotle chilis, and lime juice.
    2. Add salt for taste.
- **Shopping List**: Mayo, chipotle chilis, lime.
- **Tips**: Adjust chipotle amount for heat level.

Sesame-Ginger Dressing

- **Servings**: 1/2 cup
- **Process**:
    1. Whisk all ingredients until combined.
- **Shopping List**: Ginger, soy elixir or coconut aminos, sesame oil, honey, garlic.
- **Tips**: Perfect for Asian-inspired salads or as a dip.

- **P.T.**: 10 mins
- **Ingr.**: Duo tbsp ginger (grated), 1/4 cup soy elixir (or coconut aminos), duo tbsp sesame oil, 1 tbsp honey, tsp garlic (minced).

Roasted Bell Pepper Blend

- **P.T.**: 20 mins
- **Ingr.**: Duo red bell peppers, 1 garlic clove, 1/4 cup olive essence, salt, pepper.
- **Servings**: 1 cup
- **Process**:
  1. Oven-roast peppers, peel and deseed.
  2. Puree peppers, garlic, and olive essence.
  3. Add salt and pepper.
- **Shopping List**: Red bell peppers, garlic, olive essence.
- **Tips**: Complements grilled dishes or vegetables.

Lemon-Sesame Tahini

- **P.T.**: 10 mins
- **Ingr.**: 1/2 cup tahini, juice of 1 lemon, 1 garlic clove, water (for consistency), salt, pepper.
- **Servings**: 1 cup
- **Process**:
  1. Blend tahini, lemon juice, garlic, and water.
  2. Add salt and pepper.
- **Shopping List**: Tahini, lemon, garlic.
- **Tips**: Adjust water for desired thickness.

Sweet Balsamic Drizzle

- **P.T.**: 20 mins
- **Ingr.**: 1 cup balsamic vinegar, 1 tbsp honey.

- **Servings**: 1/2 cup
- **Process**:
    1. Simmer balsamic vinegar with honey until halved in volume.
- **Shopping List**: Balsamic vinegar, honey.
- **Tips**: Ideal over salads or roasted veggies.

Dill Cream Sauce

- **P.T.**: 10 mins
- **Ingr.**: 1/2 cup Greek yogurt (compliant), duo tbsp dill (chopped), juice of 1 lemon, salt, pepper.
- **Servings**: 1 cup
- **Process**:
    1. Combine Greek yogurt, dill, lemon juice.
    2. Season with salt and pepper.
- **Shopping List**: Greek yogurt, dill, lemon.
- **Tips**: Perfect pairing with fish or as a vegetable dip.

Spicy Avocado Cilantro Dressing

- **P.T.**: 10 mins
- **Ingr.**:
  - 2 ripe avocados
  - 1/2 cup fresh cilantro leaves
  - 1 jalapeño, seeded and chopped (optional)
  - 2 cloves garlic
  - Juice of 1 lime
  - 1/4 cup olive oil
  - Salt and pepper to taste
  - Water to thin (as needed)
- **Servings**: About 1 cup
- **Process**:

1. Blend avocados, cilantro, jalapeño, garlic, and lime juice until smooth.
2. Add olive oil, continue blending.
3. Thin with water to desired consistency, season with salt and pepper.

- **Shopping List**: Avocados, cilantro, jalapeño, garlic, lime, olive oil.
- **Tips**: Perfect as a salad dressing or a dip for vegetables. Store in an airtight container in the fridge.

Roasted Red Pepper and Walnut Pesto

- **P.T.**: 15 mins
- **Ingr.**:
  - 1 jar roasted red peppers, drained
  - 1/2 cup walnuts, toasted
  - 2 cloves garlic
  - 1/4 cup grated Parmesan cheese (optional)
  - 1/4 cup olive oil
  - Salt and pepper to taste
- **Servings**: About 1 cup
- **Process**:

1. Combine red peppers, walnuts, garlic, and Parmesan in a food processor.
2. Pulse while gradually adding olive oil.
3. Season with salt and pepper to taste.

- **Shopping List**: Roasted red peppers, walnuts, garlic, Parmesan cheese, olive oil.

- **Tips**: Serve with pasta, spread on sandwiches, or use as a dip.

Mango Lime Salsa

- **P.T.**: 20 mins
- **Ingr.**:
  - 2 ripe mangos, diced
  - Juice of 2 limes
  - 1/4 cup red onion, finely chopped
  - 1/4 cup fresh cilantro, chopped
  - 1 small red bell pepper, diced
  - Salt and pepper to taste
- **Servings**: About 2 cups
- **Process**:
  1. In a bowl, combine mangos, lime juice, red onion, cilantro, and bell pepper.
  2. Season with salt and pepper, mix well.
- **Shopping List**: Mangos, limes, red onion, cilantro, red bell pepper.
- **Tips**: Ideal as a topping for grilled fish or chicken, or as a vibrant addition to tacos.

Chapter 12: Healthy and Refreshing Beverages

Verdant Detox Concoction

- **P.T.**: 10 mins
- **Ingr.**: Duo cups spinach leaves, 1 orchard fruit (sliced), 1/2 cucumber, 1 tbsp ginger (grated), 1 cup coconut aqua, 1 tbsp citrus juice.

- **Servings**: 2
- **Process**:
    1. Blend ingredients until homogenous.
- **Shopping List**: Spinach, orchard fruit, cucumber, ginger, coconut aqua, citrus.
- **Tips**: Include ice for a chilled variant.

Almond Spice Milk

- **P.T.**: 15 mins
- **Ingr.**: Duo cups almond milk, 1 tsp cinnamon, 1/2 tsp nutmeg, 1 tbsp honey, 1 tsp vanilla essence.
- **Servings**: 2
- **Process**:
    1. Warm almond milk, stir in spices, honey, vanilla.
    2. Whisk for frothiness.
- **Shopping List**: Almond milk, cinnamon, nutmeg, honey, vanilla essence.
- **Tips**: Use a frother for enhanced creaminess.

Mint Infusion Tea

- **P.T.:** 15 mins
- **Ingr.:** 1 bunch mint, 4 cups boiling aqua, honey (optional).
- **Servings**: 4
- **Process**:
    1. Steep mint in boiling aqua for 10 mins.
    2. Strain, add honey as desired.
- **Shopping List**: Mint, honey.
- **Tips**: Enjoy either hot or over ice.

Carrot-Apple-Ginger Zest Juice

- **P.T.:** 10 mins
- **Ingr.:** Duo carrots, 1 orchard fruit, 1-inch ginger root, 1/2 citrus (juiced).
- **Servings**: 2
- **Process**:
    1. Extract juice from carrots, orchard fruit, and ginger.
    2. Stir in citrus juice.
- **Shopping List**: Carrots, orchard fruit, ginger, citrus.
- **Tips**: Modify ginger quantity for zest intensity.

Berry and Basil Fusion Smoothie

- **Servings**: 2
- **Process**:
  1. Puree berries, banana, basil, and almond milk.
- **Shopping List**: Mixed berries, banana, basil, almond milk.
- **Tips**: Freezing berries thickens the smoothie.

- **P.T.**: 10 mins
- **Ingr.**: 1 cup mixed berries, 1/2 banana, 1/4 cup basil leaves, 1 cup almond milk.

Cucumber and Citrus Water

- **P.T.**: 5 mins (+ chilling)
- **Ingr.**: 1 cucumber (sliced), Duo citrus (sliced), 4 cups aqua.
- **Servings**: 4
- **Process**:
  1. Combine cucumber, citrus, and aqua in a pitcher.
  2. Chill for at least 1 hour.
- **Shopping List**: Cucumber, citrus.
- **Tips**: Longer chilling enhances flavors.

Pineapple-Turmeric Elixir

- **P.T.**: 10 mins
- **Ingr.**: 2 cups pineapple chunks, 1-inch turmeric root, 1 cup coconut aqua, 1/2 citrus (juiced).
- **Servings**: 2
- **Process**:

1. Blend pineapple, turmeric, coconut aqua, and citrus juice.

- **Shopping List**: Pineapple, turmeric, coconut aqua, citrus.
- **Tips**: Best when served immediately.

Chia Hydration Mix

- **P.T.**: 5 mins (+ soaking)
- **Ingr.**: 2 tbsp chia seeds, 2 cups aqua, 1 tbsp lime juice, honey (to taste).
- **Servings**: 2
- **Process**:
    1. Soak chia in aqua for 30 mins.

2. Add lime and honey, stir well.

- **Shopping List**: Chia seeds, lime, honey.
- **Tips**: Can be refrigerated overnight.

Chilled Herbal Brew

- **P.T.**: 20 mins (+ cooling)
- **Ingr.**: Quartet herbal tea sachets (choice), 4 cups boiling aqua, honey (optional).
- **Servings**: 4
- **Process**:
    1. Steep tea in boiling aqua for 15 mins.
    2. Remove sachets, add honey if desired, cool.
- **Shopping List**: Herbal tea sachets, honey.
- **Tips**: Serve with ice and fresh herbs as garnish.

Watermelon-Basil Chiller

- **Process**:
    1. Blend watermelon, basil, and citrus juice until smooth.
    2. Serve over ice.
- **Shopping List**: Watermelon, basil, citrus.
- **Tips**: A perfect cooler for warm days.

- **P.T.**: 10 mins
- **Ingr.**: 4 cups watermelon (cubed), 1/4 cup basil leaves, 1/2 citrus (juiced), ice.
- **Servings**: 2

Cucumber Mint Infusion

- **P.T.**: 5 mins (+ chilling time)
- **Ingr.**:
  - 1 large cucumber, thinly sliced
  - 10-12 fresh mint leaves
  - 1 gallon of water
  - Ice (for serving)
- **Servings**: 8-10
- **Process**:
  1. In a large pitcher, combine cucumber slices, mint leaves, and water.
  2. Refrigerate for at least 1 hour, or overnight for more intense flavor.
  3. Serve chilled over ice.
- **Shopping List**: Cucumber, fresh mint, water.
- **Tips**: This beverage is perfect for hydration and detox. For a twist, add a few slices of lime or lemon.

Ginger Turmeric Wellness Shot

- **P.T.**: 15 mins
- **Ingr.**:
  - 4 inches fresh ginger root
  - 2 inches fresh turmeric root (or 1 tsp turmeric powder)
  - Juice of 2 lemons
  - 1-2 tbsp honey (optional)
  - 1 cup water
- **Servings**: 4
- **Process**:
  1. Juice ginger and turmeric roots using a juicer.
  2. Mix the juices with lemon juice, honey (if using), and water.
  3. Serve in small shot glasses.
- **Shopping List**: Ginger root, turmeric root or powder, lemons, honey, water.
- **Tips**: Consume immediately for the best nutritional benefits. Store any leftovers in the refrigerator for up to 24 hours.

Antioxidant Berry Blast Smoothie

- **P.T.**: 10 mins
- **Ingr.**:
  - 1 cup mixed berries (strawberries, blueberries, raspberries)
  - 1 banana
  - 1 cup spinach leaves
  - 1 tbsp chia seeds
  - 1 cup almond milk (or any non-dairy milk)
- **Servings**: 2
- **Process**:
  1. Blend berries, banana, spinach, chia seeds, and almond milk until smooth.
  2. Add more almond milk if needed to reach desired consistency.
- **Shopping List**: Mixed berries, banana, spinach, chia seeds, almond milk.
- **Tips**: For a colder smoothie, use frozen berries or add a few ice cubes to the blender.

Chapter 13: 30-Day Meal Plan

Day	Breakfast	Lunch	Dinner	Snack
Day 1	Avocado and Spinach Power Omelette	Mediterranean Magic Salad	Rustic Fowl & Root Vegetable Broth	Root Ensemble
Day 2	Coconut Yogurt Parfait	Avocado Citrus Delight	Spiced Lentil & Curly Kale Potage	Cauliflower Planks
Day 3	Herb-Infused Scrambled Eggs	Heirloom Tomato & Herb Salad	Hearty Ox & Sweet Tuber Soup	Asparagus with Lemon Zest
Day 4	Banana Almond Smoothie Bowl	Crunchy Kale & Apple Salad	Creamed Cauliflower & Garlic Brew	Brussels in Garlic Aroma
Day 5	Tomato Basil Frittata	Spicy Southwest Salad	Moroccan Chickpea & Veg Medley	Mushroom Ensemble
Day 6	Smashed Avocado Toast	Cucumber Noodle Salad	Smoked Tomato & Capsicum Brew	Carrot Ribbons in Citrus Glaze
Day 7	Broccoli and Egg Muffins	Broccoli Almond Crunch Salad	Ginger-Infused Gourd Soup	Beet Slices in Balsamic Veil
Day 8	Spicy Sweet Potato Hash	Sweet Potato & Pecan Salad	Zesty Fowl Citrus Soup	Green Beans with Almond Crunch
Day 9	Coconut Chia Pudding	Carrot Ribbon & Avocado Salad	Spicy Sausage & Curly Kale Stew	Eggplant Charred with Smokiness
Day 10	Carrot and Walnut Breakfast Muffins	Lemon Herb Chicken Salad	Asian Mushroom & Tofu Broth	Corn Off the Cob in Spice

Day	Breakfast	Lunch	Dinner	Snack
Day 11	Herb-Infused Scrambled Eggs	Heirloom Tomato & Herb Salad	Spiced Lentil & Curly Kale Potage	Cauliflower Planks
Day 12	Banana Almond Smoothie Bowl	Crunchy Kale & Apple Salad	Creamed Cauliflower & Garlic Brew	Asparagus with Lemon Zest
Day 13	Tomato Basil Frittata	Spicy Southwest Salad	Moroccan Chickpea & Veg Medley	Brussels in Garlic Aroma
Day 14	Smashed Avocado Toast	Cucumber Noodle Salad	Smoked Tomato & Capsicum Brew	Mushroom Ensemble
Day 15	Broccoli and Egg Muffins	Broccoli Almond Crunch Salad	Ginger-Infused Gourd Soup	Carrot Ribbons in Citrus Glaze
Day 16	Spicy Sweet Potato Hash	Sweet Potato & Pecan Salad	Zesty Fowl Citrus Soup	Beet Slices in Balsamic Veil
Day 17	Coconut Chia Pudding	Carrot Ribbon & Avocado Salad	Spicy Sausage & Curly Kale Stew	Green Beans with Almond Crunch
Day 18	Carrot and Walnut Breakfast Muffins	Lemon Herb Chicken Salad	Asian Mushroom & Tofu Broth	Eggplant Charred with Smokiness
Day 19	Avocado and Spinach Power Omelette	Mediterranean Magic Salad	Rustic Fowl & Root Vegetable Broth	Corn Off the Cob in Spice
Day 20	Coconut Yogurt Parfait	Avocado Citrus Delight	Hearty Ox & Sweet Tuber Soup	Root Ensemble

Day	Breakfast	Lunch	Dinner	Snack
Day 21	Coconut Yogurt Parfait	Avocado Citrus Delight	Creamed Cauliflower & Garlic Brew	Asparagus with Lemon Zest
Day 22	Avocado and Spinach Power Omelette	Heirloom Tomato & Herb Salad	Moroccan Chickpea & Veg Medley	Brussels in Garlic Aroma
Day 23	Coconut Chia Pudding	Crunchy Kale & Apple Salad	Smoked Tomato & Capsicum Brew	Mushroom Ensemble
Day 24	Carrot and Walnut Breakfast Muffins	Spicy Southwest Salad	Ginger-Infused Gourd Soup	Carrot Ribbons in Citrus Glaze
Day 25	Herb-Infused Scrambled Eggs	Cucumber Noodle Salad	Zesty Fowl Citrus Soup	Beet Slices in Balsamic Veil
Day 26	Banana Almond Smoothie Bowl	Broccoli Almond Crunch Salad	Spicy Sausage & Curly Kale Stew	Green Beans with Almond Crunch
Day 27	Tomato Basil Frittata	Sweet Potato & Pecan Salad	Asian Mushroom & Tofu Broth	Eggplant Charred with Smokiness
Day 28	Smashed Avocado Toast	Carrot Ribbon & Avocado Salad	Rustic Fowl & Root Vegetable Broth	Corn Off the Cob in Spice
Day 29	Broccoli and Egg Muffins	Lemon Herb Chicken Salad	Hearty Ox & Sweet Tuber Soup	Root Ensemble
Day 30	Spicy Sweet Potato Hash	Mediterranean Magic Salad	Spiced Lentil & Curly Kale Potage	Cauliflower Planks

Conclusion

As we reach the conclusion, it's important to reflect on the journey we've embarked upon together. Over the past month, you've been introduced to a myriad of recipes designed to nourish your body, invigorate your taste buds, and perhaps most importantly, to show you that healthy eating does not have to be a chore, but rather an enjoyable and sustainable part of your daily life.

Key Takeaways:

1. **Nutritional Balance:** Each recipe was crafted with the aim of providing a balance of nutrients. From the protein-packed breakfasts to the fiber-rich salads and the hearty soups and stews, the goal was always to create meals that are as nutritious as they are delicious.

2. **Simplicity in Cooking:** One of the core principles of this book was simplicity. The recipes were designed to be approachable, requiring no advanced cooking skills or hard-to-find ingredients. This simplicity, we hope, has empowered you to take control of your diet and has demystified the concept of healthy cooking.

3. **Diverse Flavors:** Through these 30 days, you've explored flavors from around the world, each bringing its unique nutritional profile and health benefits. This diversity not only makes your meals more enjoyable but also ensures a wider range of vitamins and minerals in your diet.

4. **Mindful Eating:** The journey with whole foods is as much about developing a mindful approach to eating as it is about the foods themselves. By focusing on whole, unprocessed ingredients, you've taken a step towards understanding and appreciating the food you consume and its impact on your body.

5. **Sustainable Lifestyle Change:** Lastly, this cookbook was not intended as a one-off experience but as a stepping stone towards a long-term, sustainable change in how you view and interact with food. The skills, recipes, and knowledge you've gained are tools that will serve you well beyond these 30 days.

Moving Forward:

- Continue exploring and experimenting with whole foods. Use the skills and confidence you've gained to try new ingredients and recipes.
- Remember the importance of moderation and balance. It's okay to indulge occasionally; what matters most is the overall pattern of your diet.
- Share your experience and knowledge with others. Cooking is a joy that's multiplied when shared.

In closing, thank you for allowing this cookbook to be a part of your whole food journey. May the habits and lessons you've learned carry you forward towards a healthier, happier you. Remember, every meal is an opportunity to nourish not just your body, but also your soul. Keep exploring, keep cooking, and keep thriving!

Measurement Conversion Table

Volume Measurements

US Measurement	Metric Measurement
1 teaspoon (tsp)	5 milliliters (ml)
1 tablespoon (tbsp)	15 milliliters (ml)
1 fluid ounce (fl oz)	30 milliliters (ml)
1 cup (C.)	240 milliliters (ml)
1 pint (2 Cs)	470 milliliters (ml)
1 quart (4 Cs)	0.95 liters (L)
1 gallon (16 Cs)	3.8 liters (L)

Weight Measurements

US Measurement	Metric Measurement
1 ounce (oz)	28 grams (g)
1 pound (lb)	450 grams (g)
1 pound (lb)	0.45 kilograms (kg)

Length Measurements

US Measurement	Metric Measurement
1 inch (in)	2.54 centimeters (cm)
1 foot (ft)	30.48 centimeters (cm)
1 foot (ft)	0.3048 meters (m)
1 yard (yd)	0.9144 meters (m)

Temperature Conversions

Fahrenheit (°F)	Celsius (°C)
32°F	0°C
212°F	100°C
Formula: (°F - 32) x 0.5556 = °C	Formula: (°C x 1.8) + 32 = °F

Oven Temperature Conversions

US Oven Term	Fahrenheit (°F)	Celsius (°C)
Very Slow	250°F	120°C
Slow	300-325°F	150-165°C
Moderate	350-375°F	175-190°C
Moderately Hot	400°F	200°C
Hot	425-450°F	220-230°C
Very Hot	475-500°F	245-260°C

Made in the USA
Columbia, SC
27 October 2024

45141778R00067